&CARLTON CHRONICLES

CARLTON CHRONICLES

Text by Francis M. Carroll
Photo Editing by Marlene Wisuri
& the Carlton History Committee

Carlton County Historical Society
Cloquet, Minnesota

ISBN 10 0-9618959-1-8
      13 978-0-9618959-1-4

Printed and bound in the United States of America
by Bang Printing, Brainerd, Minnesota
Book layout and design by Marlene Wisuri

The
minnesota
humanities
COMMISSION

The publication of *Carlton Chronicles* is made possible in part with funding from the Minnesota Humanities Commission in cooperation with the National Endowment for the Humanities. The 125th Anniversary Celebration of Carlton has been designated a *We the People* project by the National Endowment for the Humanities (NEH). NEH's *We the People* initiative supports projects that examine the history, accomplishments, and culture of the United States.

National Endowment for the Humanities

WE the People

Sharing the lessons of history with all Americans.

Carlton County Historical Society
406 Cloquet Avenue
Cloquet, MN 55720
218/879-1938
www.carltoncountyhs.org

℘ DONORS TO CARLTON CHRONICLES

Financial assistance for the publication of this book came from many individuals, businesses, government entities, and civic organizations. We are very grateful for their contributions.

Major gifts of $500 and over were given by ~
Carlton Area Chamber of Commerce
Carlton Lions Club
Carlton Redevelopment
City of Carlton
Colymbus Foundation (Nancy Bagley)
        In Memory of Avis Woodworth Hursh
Matteson, Richard & Philip
        In Memory of John August Johnson & Alma Abramson Spjuth Johnson & their ten children—
        Annie, Augie, Freddy, Sago, Mabel Wiehe, Albert, Brenny, Dolly, Horner, Edy Matteson &
        Baby Lawrence

Gifts of $100 - $500 were given by ~
Anderson, Ben
Beckstrom, Larry & Carol
Benson, Sheryl
Bergum, Donald
        In Memory of Ted & Gerda Bergum
Embers Restaurant
Filiatrault, Tom; Filiatrault, Gerry; Filiatrault-Laine, Jeanne; Lovas, Kathy; Heilman, Barbara;
        In Memory of Elizabeth & Michael Brady, Rose Brady Johnson & Margaret Brady
Gravelle, Barbara
        In Memory of Jewell Hinz Anderson
Haubner, C. Brooke
        In Memory of Cliff & Marge Haubner
Haubner, Mike & Liz
Jim's Lawn Service
Johnson, Norman & Karen
Johnson, Tim & Ruby
Knox, John & Karen
        In Memory of John August Johnson & Alma Abramson Johnson
Korpela, Barbara
        In Memory of Edmund C. Hargest, Wilhelmina G. Hargest & Robert W. Hargest
Melin (Dahlberg), Donna
Northland Funeral Home
Nygren, Dick & Patricia
        In Honor of Albert C. & Doris H. Johnson
Olson, Ruth V.
        In Memory of Robert E. Olson
Powers Barbershop
Randelin, Denny & Becky
Rodd, Robert and Leola
Rotary Club of Cloquet
Schiedermayer, Jeanne
        In Memory of her husband, Phil
State Bank of Carlton
Town of Twin Lakes
Tribby, Bob & Judy
Wells Fargo Bank - Carlton - Cloquet

DEDICATION

This book is dedicated to all of the
Carlton pioneers who labored
together to form a community.

CARLTON HISTORY COMMITTEE

Ben Anderson
Larry Beckstrom
Dick Chick
Mike Haubner
Norm Johnson
Ron Johnson
Ruby Johnson
Tim Johnson
Barb Korpela
Donna Melin
Darold Powers
Leola Rodd

Heartfelt thanks go to those Carlton residents, former residents, and their families for sorting through family archives in order to share information, send clippings, and provide photographs which have added greatly to the depth and interest of this book.

ABOUT THE PHOTOS:

Unless otherwise indicated, all photographs are from the collection of the Carlton County Historical Society. Photographers are credited when known. Photos loaned to CCHS for this book are credited as such. Several photos were contributed by more than one person, but are credited to only one. Minnesota Historical Society materials are used with permission and credited by the abbreviation MHS.

Cover Photos
Front cover: Carlton Post Card, ca. 1910, courtesy of Pam Ziebarth
Back cover: Top - Great Northern Railroad Bridge, photo by Thomas Huse
        Middle - Carlton Sign, photo by Tim Johnson
        Bottom - Jay Cooke State Park, photo by Allen Anway

CONTENTS

꧁ INTRODUCTION

When I look at the abstract for my property at Chub Lake, the history of Carlton and Twin Lakes Township jumps off the pages—The Lake Superior & Mississippi Railroad Company; J. Edgar Thomson and William G. Moorhead trustees in a suit; the Saint Paul & Duluth Railroad Company; James M. Paine & W.W. McNair; Asa and Bertha Paine; Sauntry-Cain Company; Cordelia Ayer Paine; Henry Oldenburg; C.I. McNair; and so on, through the years. These are the companies and people that shaped Carlton and Carlton County from the 1860s right into the twentieth century. This is an experience that everyone in the Carlton area who owns a bit of land must share—our ownership of those echoes from the past.

Carlton has played a unique role and has had a distinctive history. I have found it to be a wonderful story. Carlton the railway hub, the sawmill town, the farm service center, the county seat. And the story is filled with fascinating and engaging people—railroaders, lumbermen, public servants, grand dames, business women, inn-keepers, entrepreneurs, nere-do-wells, war heroes, Yankees, Ulstermen, French-Canadians, Germans, Swedes, Finns, and more. What a cast of characters. Who could have invented Cordelia Ayer Paine and her sister Madame Blandin? What more could we learn about the origins of the lumber industry from Captain Paine or from William Martin Cain? What of those many immigrants from Canada—French and Irish? And how curious I was about those Ulstermen from Six Mile Cross, County Tyrone. Would that we knew all these lives from rich, full biographies. I have only scratched the surface of the history of Carlton, but I hope I have conveyed some of the wonderful breadth and complexity and charm of that history.

Every book is the product of many hands, and it is a pleasure for me to acknowledge the encouragement and help that has been given to me in preparing the text for this book. First of all I am indebted to the Carlton History Committee for inviting me to have a part in the One Hundred and Twenty-five Year Anniversary Project to produce a history of the community. I was flattered to be asked and delighted to participate. It is also a great pleasure to have an opportunity to work once again with Marlene Wisuri and the Carlton County Historical Society. Marlene's professionalism and expertise make every project with which she is involved a great success. Marlene and her staff provided me with vast amounts of photocopied materials, and sent off microfilms of the *Carlton County Vidette,* allowing me to do much of the research for this project here in Winnipeg. The Minnesota Historical Society and their manuscript and archival resources were also a valuable source of documentary information with which to reconstruct the history of the town and the county. Ruth Bauer Anderson and Deborah Miller were, as usual, of great help and understanding in guiding me through the elaborate collections in the holdings of MHS. Similarly, my friend Julia Wallace, Head of Government Documents at the University of Minnesota Library, came to my assistance once again, opening to me the resources of that great institution. In my own institution, the University of Manitoba, Barbara Bennell, Supervisor of Document Delivery, facilitated my acquisition of material from other libraries, and Sandra Ferguson and Carol Adams made available to me the microfilm reader in the History Department. Séamus Cain, in the process of writing a biography of his grandfather, William Martin Cain, shared with me both his vast information about his grandfather and the lumber industry and also many very helpful suggestions of where I might look for documentary material in the Minnesota Historical Society. The history of Carlton and the forest industry in Minnesota will be greatly enriched when his own studies are published. I have also traded on several old friendships, getting advice on railroads from Thomas N. Huse, the Carlton he remembered from John Kalbrener, recollections of Mrs. Guy C. Smith from Karen Hanson Christenson, and consulting about recent Carlton history from Donald and Gale Brown, Denny and Ann Sauter, and Vicki and Dean Kerttula. Many thanks to all of these people who have helped make this book possible.

Francis M. Carroll

East

Carlton as seen from the air on July 23,1981

North

South

West

℘ PUBLISHER'S PREFACE

The publication of *Carlton Chronicles* brings me a great deal of personal satisfaction. It has long been a goal of mine to get the important history of Carlton into print. Carlton not only has an interesting and colorful past, its history is of importance to a much larger area and audience because of railroad, lumbering, electric power, and Jay Cooke State Park stories. It is especially gratifying to have Dr. Francis Carroll bring this history alive with such a vivid text. Dr. Carroll was the author of the first book of Carlton County history published in 1987 by the Carlton County Historical Society—*Crossroads in Time: A History of Carlton County, Minnesota. Crossroads* set a standard for local history writing that is much respected in the field. We refer to it often when answering research requests and introducing new readers to Carlton County history. Dr. Carroll also authored *Reflections of Our Past: A Pictorial History of Carlton County* for the Society and, with Franklin Raiter, *Fires of Autumn: The Cloquet-Moose Lake Disaster of 1918* for the Minnesota Historical Society Press. He brings a wide breadth of knowledge and insight to each publication.

Another pleasure in doing *Carlton Chronicles* has been getting to know more members of the Carlton community and working with the Carlton History Committee. Darold Powers has collected Carlton history for years making Powers Barbershop a repository of community history. He provided the inspiration for the book project. CCHS Board member, Tim Johnson, has ably chaired the committee, holding numerous meetings and helping to gather photographs and other material. The meetings were lively events that included much reminiscing about life in Carlton usually set off by sharing old photographs. The committee has not only gathered valuable material for the book, but also spearheaded efforts to raise money for its publication.

Support for the book came in many forms and from many people. We are appreciative of the support provided the project by the Minnesota Humanities Commission and the many financial donors. The Minnesota Historical Society provided rare vintage photographs. CCHS staff members, Roberta Malwitz and Harriette Niemi, covered many hours at the Center while the book was in production and provided proofreading, research assistance, and encouragement. Kris Hiller at Jay Cooke Park provided scans of needed photographs, and Maryanne Norton at the Duluth Public Library assisted with research.

This book joins eight other books, several educational pamphlets, a cookbook, and a CD published by the Society. Through our publishing program we further our mission of collecting, preserving, and disseminating the history of Carlton County. We hope you will enjoy this latest offering which provides a glimpse into the history of Carlton in words and pictures.

Marlene Wisuri
Director, Carlton County Historical Society

Residents of Carlton danced in the streets in August of 1949.
In the background stands the office of the *Carlton County Vidette,*
the newspaper which chronicled activities in Carlton, great and
small, for some eighty years.

In a spirit of celebration we offer this look at Carlton's history of
the last 125 years and more.

Page No. 1

⁊

SCHEDULE 1.—Inhabitants in _R. R. Junction_, in the County of _Carlton_, State of _Minnesota_; enumerated by me on the _29th_ day of _July_, 1870.

Post Office: _Thompson_ _John D. Wilcox_, Ass't Marshal.

1	2	3 The name of every person whose place of abode on the first day of June, 1870, was in this family.	4	5	6	7 Profession, Occupation, or Trade of each person, male or female.	8 Value of Real Estate	9 Value of Personal Estate	10 Place of Birth, naming State or Territory of U.S.; or the Country, if of foreign birth.	11	12	13	14	15	16	17	18 Whether deaf and dumb, blind, insane, or idiotic.	19	20
1	1	Columbus H.	23	M	W	??			Canada E	/	/								
		Arthur Roger	20	M	W	Laborer			Canada W	/	/								
		Harwood Dwight	19	M	W	Laborer			New York										
		Harwood Napoleon	17	M	W	Laborer			Canada E	/	/								
		Lennox B	24	M	W	Carpenter			Canada E	/	/								
2	2	Murphy John	28	M	W	Restaurant Keeper		300	Hamburg	/	/							1	
3	3	Wells Scott	23	M	W	Laborer	400		Canada W	/	/							1	
		Shea William	22	M	W	Laborer	200		New York									1	
		McCarty H	12	M	W	Laborer			Massachusetts									1	
4	4	Matthew Henry	33	M	W	Saloon Keeper		120	England	/	/							1	
		Henry Peter	26	M	W	Saloon Keeper			Scotland	/	/								
5	5	Knapp Henry	31	M	W	Saloon Keeper			Wirtenburg	/	/						1	
		Terson Philip	30	M	W	Saloon Keeper	100		Prussia	/	/							1	
6	6	McGee John	26	M	W	Saloon Keeper	430		Pennsylvania	/	/							1	
		" Michael	21	M	W	Saloon Keeper		300	Pennsylvania	/	/							1	
7	7	Scott James	24	M	W	Grocer		300	New York									1	
		Shearer L. W.	24	M	W	Iron Merchant	400	1000	Canada E	/	/							1	
		French Frank	11	M	W	Laborer			Minnesota										
		McCarty E	14	M	W	Cook			Minnesota										
		Fry J	23	M	W	Butcher		800	Massachusetts									1	

A portion of the 1870 census of Railroad Junction as recorded by John D. Wilcox on the 29th of July, 1870.

12

CHAPTER ONE

A Clearing in the Wilderness

For most of us the history of the town of Carlton begins with the famous photograph of a group of men in coats, neckties, and white shirts, standing in the wilderness on a bright winter's day, ready to turn the first shovel full of earth to launch construction of the Northern Pacific Railroad. The wheelbarrow, pick, and shovel are in front of them ready to do the job. Out of sight, the fire, needed to melt the snow and thaw the earth to be turned, has already been lit. Sightseers have ridden over by sleigh from Twin Lakes to witness the event—Mr. and Mrs. John Dunphy and Misses Annie Bardon and Philomena McCormick—and they must have shivered in the cold waiting for the camera to be set up and the important visitors to be arranged in line. The dignitaries—the future mayor of Duluth, the city attorney of Superior, the editor of the Duluth newspaper, the special correspondent from Philadelphia, the former Confederate civil engineer for the railroad, the former owner of the stage-coach line from Duluth to St. Paul, the telegraph operator from Fond du Lac—came to launch the second great transcontinental railroad in the United States, one of the most ambitious enterprises of the 1870s. And the railroad built the town, Northern Pacific Junction, as it was first called, as it did so many other towns and settlements across the northern tier of the United States. Few towns or institutions anywhere can have had such a visibly documented event out of which they have grown and prospered. The dignitaries and sightseers came to witness the launching of the great railroad enterprise, but in fact they were also participating in the founding of the town that would create a life of its own and outlive the railroad. Of course, history did not begin on Tuesday, February 15, 1870, and to understand the emergence of the

Photograph taken at commencement of work on the Northern Pacific Railroad at N. P. Junction, now Carlton, Minnesota, February 15th 1870.

The beginning of work on the Northern Pacific Railroad, February 15, 1870. Railroad officials and dignitaries from both Duluth and Superior had to melt the snow to get to the earth, but the Chief Engineer could cable Jay Cooke: "Ground broke on Northern Pacific Railroad today." Colonel Joshua B. Culver, soon to be mayor of Duluth, turned the first shovel, and Colonel Hiram Hayes, the mayor of Superior, pushed the wheelbarrow in an early gesture of Twin Ports solidarity in this great enterprise. Prayers were said by two clergymen. Dr. Thomas Foster, editor of the *Duluth Minnesotian*, stands bareheaded in the center.

town of Carlton we must look beyond the famous photograph to the events and circumstances that made possible the growth and importance of the settlement.

The history of Carlton County precedes the town of Carlton by almost fifteen years. Named for Reuben B. Carlton, the government blacksmith to the Fond du Lac Indians, regional promoter, and a senator in the state legislature, Carlton County was created on May 23, 1857, from part of St. Louis County, while Minnesota was still a Territory. Indeed, the Minnesota Territory, detached from Wisconsin when the latter became a state in 1848, was formed into a Territory in 1849 and entered the Federal Union as a state in 1858. In fact, the county's political life was quite problematical, inasmuch as it had almost no settlers. The region really required a modern, practical means of transportation before it could attract settlers. Of course, the St. Louis River had been a means of transportation early in the nineteenth century and before. The Ojibwe and the Sioux before them had lived along the river and used it as a route into the hinterland. European explorers used the river seeking passages to the Mississippi River and the Rainy River and access to the center of North America, beginning with Daniel Greysolon, Sieur DuLhut in 1679 and continuing right up to Governor Lewis Cass and Henry Rowe Schoolcraft in the 1820s and 1830s. Fur traders, similarly, used the St. Louis River to gain access to the Native people and as the transportation system to carry their furs out of the wilderness to the eastern markets. The St. Louis River, however, with its dramatic and beautiful rapids and long and extremely difficult portages, could not meet the modern transportation needs of settlers and farmers.

In the early summer of 1679 Daniel Greysolon, Sieur duLhut, having proceeded from New France in the previous months, became the first European known to ascend the St. Louis River and pass through the region of Carlton and Thomson. DuLhut may have been preceded by Etienne Brulé as early as 1629 or Pierre-Esprit Radisson and Médart Chouart des Groseillies in 1659, but there are no records. The scene here is depicted by the distinguished Minnesota artist, naturalist, and author, Francis Lee Jaques.   Oil Painting - MHS, ca. 1922

Henry Rowe Schoolcraft, Indian Agent, scientist, and ethnologist, traveled up the St. Louis River on three occasions. In 1820 he explored, with Governor Lewis Cass, the extent of the upper Mississippi River. In 1826 he was with a party that negotiated a treaty with the area Ojibwe at Fond du Lac, and in 1832 he led an expedition to identify the source of the Mississippi River.
Photo - MHS, ca. 1855

Fur traders and other travelers faced difficult portages on the St. Louis River as seen in this photo of men portaging a large birch bark canoe.   Photo - MHS, ca. 1880

During the War of 1812 much of the western Great Lakes region was lost to the United States, seized by British troops, fur traders, and Indians. American diplomats effectively recovered the area for the United States in the peace negotiations. Following that war the government attempted to assert its sovereignty and establish a presence in the northwest by building a series of forts at various strategic points, of which Fort Snelling, built in 1819, was a major establishment. A second part of that program was the building of military roads connecting these forts with the frontier region. In 1850 Congress passed legislation providing for a series of military roads radiating out from Fort Snelling, including a road from Point Douglas, at the confluence of the St. Croix and Mississippi rivers, to the St. Louis River. This "Military Road" would link Lake Superior with the Mississippi River and Fort Snelling. Not until 1858 was the road fully completed, working its way through Carlton County to Superior, Wisconsin, with a side road north to the St. Louis River, through what is now Wrenshall, to roughly the point where Otter Creek enters the St. Louis opposite Thomson. Mail service on horseback was started in 1856—once a week to Superior, increasing to three times a week in 1863. By 1867 and 1868 requests were made from Duluth, Oneota, and Fond du Lac that their postal service also be routed through Twin Lakes. Regular stagecoach service was not provided until 1861. Originally it took six days and cost $35.00, but with the Burbank, Merriam & Co. line, and improvements to the road, the time was cut to three days costing between $10.00 and $15.00, plus food and accommodations. The teams of horses varied between four and six and were changed some fourteen times during the trip.

Almost every commentator complained that the road was the worst they had ever experienced, with rough corduroy, steep hills, and never ending mud, and one historian concluded that it remained in a "permanently unfinished condition." Nevertheless, James S. Ritchie, writing in 1857, assured his readers that "the military road from Superior to Point Douglas, on the Mississippi River, is in an excellent condition, and teams are daily passing over it;" hundreds were arriving in Superior over the road, he said. Stagecoaches required stops to change horses and refresh passengers and in Carlton County stations were built at Elkton (near Moose Lake), Blackhoof, and Twin Lakes (now known as Scotts Corner). Of these stations, Twin Lakes was the largest. For people heading south Twin Lakes was the first stop, a chance for food and an opportunity to stretch one's legs while the horses were being changed; for people heading east toward Fond du Lac or Superior, Twin Lakes might be their last overnight stay on the trip from St. Paul. The hearty breakfasts, cakes, and pies cooked by Mrs. Chengwatana Smith and Mrs. McIntyre were remembered for years. With a post office, tavern, and general store operated by Stephen Dunphy, known as Dunphy's Trading Post and Stage Stop, as well as the largest white population, it is not surprising that when Carlton County was formed in 1857 Twin Lakes was made the county seat.

The Military Road

"How shall I describe to you our experiences? It was the roughest, pleasantest, most agreeable, most terrible, muddiest and most miserably romantic journey on the whole which any of us had ever undertaken ... Now a horse was down, now a king bolt broke, then some part of the harness gave way. Often a wagon stuck in a hole and had to be lifted out by strong hands at the wheels and a driver at a sudden jolt left his seat and, describing a complete summersault forward, alighted on his back in the mud face toward Heaven and pipe in mouth still industriously smoking ... The road beat, I verily believe, in utter unmitigated badness all the bad roads not altogether unpassable since the deluge."

A Duluth correspondent in the *Philadelphia Inquirer*, August 16, 1869, cited in Ellis Paxson Oberholtzer, *Jay Cooke: Financier of the Civil War* (New York: Augustus M. Kelly, 1968 [first published, 1907]), vol. II, p. 1.

"On the 26th of June [1870] I quitted the shores of Lake Superior and made my way back to Moose Lake. Without exception, the road thither was the very worst I had ever travelled over—four horses essayed to drag a stage-waggon over, or rather, I should say, through, a track of mud and ruts impossible to picture. The stage fare amounted to $6, or £1, 4 s. for 34 miles. An extra dollar reserved the box-seat and gave me the double advantage of knowing what was coming in the rut line and taking another lesson in the idiom of the American stage-driver. This idiom consists of the smallest possible amount of dictionary words, a few Scriptural names rather irreverently used, a very large intermixture of 'git-ups' and ejaculator 'hi's,' and a general tendency to blasphemy all round."

William Francis Butler, *The Great Lone Land: A Narrative of Travel and Adventure in the North West of America* (Edmonton: M.G. Hurtig, Ltd., 1968 [first published, 1872]), p. 76.

One of the oldest structures in the county, the old stage stop hotel now serves as a hospitality center for meetings, weddings, and parties. This hotel at Twin Lakes was one of the links on the Military Road built from Point Douglas (where the St. Croix River joins the Mississippi River) to the St. Louis River and Superior. The road functioned as the main transportation route north and south from the 1850s until it was superseded by the railroad in the 1870s.

By the 1850s the technological innovation that captured the imagination of people across the United States was the railroad. The inadequacies and inconveniences of travel on surfaces like the Military Road were obvious to everyone. The 1850s saw the chartering of countless railroads across the country, no less so in the Minnesota Territory. It is worth noting that on May 23, 1857, when Carlton County was created, the territorial legislature also chartered several companies, two being railroads. One of those, the Nebraska & Lake Superior Railroad, was to connect the head of the lakes to St. Paul and Nebraska. (Reuben Carlton was also one of the people listed in the incorporation.)

The financial Panic of 1857 and the outbreak of the Civil War in 1861 meant that many of these grandiose railroad plans never materialized. However, despite these national issues, and rivalries from both Wisconsin (Milwaukee and Bayfield) and Minnesota (Anoka and St. Cloud), the building of a railroad from southern Minnesota to Lake Superior was not allowed to languish. In 1861 the name was changed to the Lake Superior & Mississippi Railroad and grading began near St. Paul in 1864, although it was not until 1868 that the first thirty miles of track were laid down. Construction also began in Duluth, through Fond du Lac, and up the rocky passes along the Dalles of the St. Louis River through what is now Jay Cooke State Park. Through steep cuts and over five large ravines (one being over one hundred feet deep) on magnificent wooden trestles, the tracks wound their way to what became the new village of Thomson, named after J. Edgar Thomson, president of the Pennsylvania Railroad and a director of the Lake Superior & Mississippi. In 1869 Robert Ownes built the first house in Thomson and by 1870 the settlement was booming, with the tracks coming up from Fond du Lac, the bridge over the St. Louis River completed, sidings for locomotives, cars, and supplies, and a variety of shanties and buildings.

Wooden trestle of the Lake Superior & Mississippi Railroad. This photograph illustrates the enormous engineering and maintenance problems involved in building the original track along the St. Louis River valley in what is now Jay Cooke State Park.　　　Photo by Gaylord & Thompson - MHS

On August 1, 1870, the last spike was driven near Thomson on the Lake Superior & Mississippi Railroad linking St. Paul with Duluth. The first through train, consisting of a locomotive, baggage car, two passenger coaches, and two freight cars, started from the St. Paul station that day at 7:15 in the morning and arrived in Duluth at 11:30 at night, making the 154 mile trip in 16 hours and 15 minutes (at not quite 10 miles per hour). At long last the job was done. The *Duluth Minnesotian* claimed that the event was "the most important in the history of the state." The president of the railroad and other dignitaries—including Supreme Court Chief Justice and President Lincoln's former

Secretary of the Treasury, Salmon P. Chase; Governor William R. Marshall; Jay Cooke's partner, William G. Moorhead; and other officers of the company—would make a ceremonial trip later, but there must have been spontaneous celebrations all along the line as that first train rolled through. Within a year the time from St. Paul to Duluth was reduced to twelve hours and progress was made as the equipment and the tracks were improved, although it was claimed by some that L.S. & M. meant "Long, Slow & Miserable." However, on August 14, 1891, the tracks were cleared and engineer Jim Root, who had driven locomotives for General William T. Sherman in the Civil War and was later the hero of the Hinckley Fire disaster, at the throttle of engine Number 69 set a speed record of three hours and twenty minutes from St. Paul to Duluth. People came out to watch that morning as he took his train through Carlton at an impressive fifty-five miles an hour.

A Lake Superior & Mississippi Railroad locomotive. The man standing in the engine cab is Jim Root, who drove the record-breaking train from St. Paul to Duluth on August 14, 1891, and who later became the hero of the Hinckley Fire in 1894.
Photo from Runk Collection - MHS

The Lake Superior & Mississippi Railroad suffered in the Panic of 1873 and eventually went into bankruptcy. It was reorganized as the St. Paul & Duluth Railroad on July 17, 1877. During this period many of its lease arrangements with the Northern Pacific Railroad were broken, although the shared and jointly owned facilities were maintained. On June 15, 1900, the Northern Pacific took over the St. Paul & Duluth, acquiring all of the track and facilities and integrating them into its system.

Andreas M. Miller, of Duluth, and several others quickly built sawmills in Thomson to exploit the timber resources of the St. Louis River, not to mention the capacity to ship the finished lumber out on the new railroad. The St. Louis Slate and Brick Company later built facilities on the river to exploit the waterpower to grind slate for the production of between 8 and 10 million bricks a year. Stagecoach service was terminated in 1871, and travel on the old Military Road declined. Twin Lakes lost its premier position in the county.

Andreas M. Miller operated successful sawmills first in Duluth and then in Thomson. ca. 1877
Photo - Northeast Minnesota Historical Center

With the population so small and communications so difficult, Carlton County had really functioned as an administrative district of St. Louis County from 1857 until 1870. However, recognizing the importance of the new railroad and commercial center, the state legislature changed the county seat to Thomson on February 18, 1870, and created provisions for the election, in May, of two County Commissioners, a Sheriff, a Coroner, a Treasurer, an Auditor, and a Register of Deeds. On September 26, 1870, the Board of County Commissioners held their first meeting in Thomson and created the townships of Thomson, Twin Lakes, and Moose Lake. This marked the beginning of organized government in Carlton County.

Thomson about 1885, showing houses built on the bedrock. Photo - MHS

Thomson

"What Manchester is to London, Lowell to Boston, so will the City of Thomson be to Duluth. It is situated on the Saint Louis River, about twenty-three miles Southwest from this city, but eight miles above Fond du Lac, to which latter place that river is navigable. Here will be the junction of the Lake Superior and Northern Pacific Railroads, which, of itself will create a considerable business. The line of the former road from Duluth to the Dalles forms part of the latter road, so we can reasonably predict that this place will become at once a center of great business activity."

Anon., *Duluth: Its Location in the United States and its Commanding Position on the Highway of Trade Between the Territories of the Northwest and the Atlantic Cities, and of the Commerce Between Asia and the Eastern States and Europe* (Duluth: Tribune Printing Company, 1871), p. 41.

The planing mill
of Andreas M.
Miller at
Thomson,
about 1885.

Photo - MHS

Sawmill and crew of the
Andreas M. Miller
Lumber Company at
Thomson about 1874.

The slate brick plant at
Thomson, built by the Jay
Cooke interests in the 1890s.
The plant used waterpower
to grind the slate into the
mud with which they made
what was regarded as a
superior brick. The founda-
tions for the plant can still
be seen among the rocks
below the dam. The plant is
shown here with the St. Louis
River in flood conditions.

Colonel Reuben B. Carlton

Reuben Carlton was born on March 4, 1812, in Onondaga County, New York, and by 1845 was employed by the United States government as a blacksmith in the service of the Lake Superior Ojibwe at Fond du Lac. In those years Colonel Carlton (the title was honorific) and his wife Susan, also from New York State, lived in a two-room log cabin and were respected for their hospitality. Carlton saw the potential of the northern Minnesota region. He assisted the United States Geological Survey expedition along the North Shore of Lake Superior (and had a 1,526 foot summit along the North Shore named after him), and he was also associated with various mining projects in the region. In fact, during the 1850s Carlton became involved in numerous projects to develop the area, from plank roads to canals opening up the Duluth harbor to a possible canal linking Lake Superior with the Mississippi River by way of Sandy Lake to the chartering of the Lake Superior & Crow Wing Railroad. Nothing came of these schemes at the time, but Carlton was also one of the incorporators of the Nebraska & Lake Superior Railroad, which in 1861 became the Lake Superior & Mississippi Railroad and by 1870 linked St. Paul with Duluth by way of Northern Pacific Junction (later called Carlton). In 1857 the territorial legislature created several counties, one of them named for Reuben Carlton. The following year Carlton was himself elected to the new Minnesota state senate. Carlton died on December 6, 1863, and is buried in the Nemadji Cemetery in Superior. His wife Susan died on April 6, 1869, and is buried next to him.

Colonel Reuben B. Carlton was the government blacksmith to the Fond du Lac Ojibwe. Carlton came to Fond du Lac in 1845 and became a leading promoter of the region and its potential for railroad development. In 1857, the newly created Carlton County was named after him by the Minnesota Territorial Legislature. Carlton was elected to the state senate when Minnesota became the 32nd state in 1858.

Larry Luukkonen, *Reuben B. Carlton: Frontier Blacksmith and Visionary* (Cloquet: Carlton County Historical Society, 2005).
James A. Thorp, "Reuben Carlton's namesake," *Duluth News-Tribune*, February 4, 1979.

Sources:
Carroll, Francis M. *Crossroads in Time: A History of Carlton County, Minnesota.* Cloquet: Carlton County Historical Society, 1987.
Fritzen, John. *The History of Fond du Lac and Jay Cooke Park.* Duluth: St. Louis County Historical Society, 1978.
King, Frank A. "Railroads at the Head of the Lakes," in Ryck Lydecker and Lawrence Sommer (eds.), *Duluth, Sketches of the Past: A Bicentennial Collection.* Duluth: American Revolutionary War Bicentennial Commission, 1976.
Luukkonen, Larry. *Reuben B. Carlton: Frontier Blacksmith and Visionary.* Cloquet: Carlton County Historical Society, 2005.
Prosser, Richard S. *Rails to the North Star: One Hundred Years of Railroad Evolution in Minnesota.* Minneapolis: Dillon Press, 1966.
Ritchie, James S. *Wisconsin and Its Resources; With Lake Superior, Its Commerce and Navigation.* Philadelphia: Charles Desilver, 1857.
Singley, Grover. *Tracing Minnesota's Old Government Roads.* St. Paul: Minnesota Historical Society, 1974.

Northern Pacific Junction about 1882, with a load of logs steaming through.

Carlton about 1899 as seen from the rocks east of town, with the feed mill to the left.

CHAPTER 2

Building a Railroad

The building of the Northern Pacific Railroad was a major national enterprise. The Union Pacific and Central Pacific—the first transcontinental railways—were completed in 1869, and the nation thrilled at the linking of the east and west coasts by rail. Long before this a northern transcontinental had been proposed, and in 1864, the midst of the Civil War, President Abraham Lincoln signed the charter for the Northern Pacific. The prospect of trade with the Far East was as promising then as it is now, quite apart from the opening up of the northwest and the domestic traffic such a railroad would carry. However, unlike many of the eastern railroads that were built through already settled country, the Northern Pacific would be striking out through the northern tier of the United States, where there were almost no white settlers—no customers—toward its goal on the west coast. The financing of this kind of operation depended on enormous government land grants, huge private loans, and a lot of luck. Both the federal and state governments provided the land grants; Jay Cooke, the Philadelphia banker who had financed the government's debt during the Civil War, provided the money; but the matter of luck would be more uncertain.

Jay Cooke was at the height of his power and prestige after the Civil War when he developed a strong interest in the potential for the head of the lakes region, and he may just have regretted not having a share in the success of the first transcontinental. By 1868 he visited Duluth and began buying property in the settlement and timberland in Carlton and St. Louis Counties. In 1865 he had been approached by the president of the Lake Superior & Mississippi Railroad, William L. Banning, to sell its bonds, and in 1869 he agreed to do so and also to acquire bonds on his own account. This was a major commitment to the railroad. At the same time Cooke had been cool to the appeals of the president of the Northern Pacific in 1865, perhaps because his bank was still preoccupied with servicing government bonds. In 1869, with investments in the region and also in the Lake Superior & Mississippi Railroad, and having been passed

Jay Cooke, the Philadelphia banker who undertook to finance the building of the Northern Pacific Railroad. By 1873 he went bankrupt and lost control of the railroad. However, he was able to recover his finances sufficiently to repurchase many of his Minnesota investments, including the old railroad right of way along the St. Louis River from Thomson to Fond du Lac. This was eventually developed into the Thomson dam and Forbay hydroelectric project. Cooke's heirs donated much of the river valley to the state to be developed as Jay Cooke State Park.   Photo - MHS

over for Secretary of the Treasury by President Ulysses S. Grant, Cooke was much more interested in the Northern Pacific. The Northern Pacific was such a vast undertaking, however, that several of his partners were anxious about the difficulties of a single bank financing such a project. After devising several financial plans, Cooke was able to persuade his colleagues and on January 1, 1870, he had worked out the terms with the president of the railroad, J. Gregory Smith. While the agreement was complicated, Cooke was able to inform Smith on 24 January that he had raised $5,600,000 to build the railroad to the Red River and that construction could begin as soon as possible. Engineers had made several surveys of the possible routes for the northern railroad, and politicians and interest groups had made various claims about where the railroad should start and what its route ought to be. Strong arguments had been made for a terminus at Ashland, Bayfield, or Superior, Wisconsin. However, the commitment of the Lake Superior & Mississippi to a terminus at Duluth and the fact that its construction was well under way, together with the investments of Cooke and his partners in both Duluth and the Lake Superior road, meant that the Northern Pacific would capitalize on these existing facilities and make Duluth its terminus.

William L. Banning was president of the Lake Superior & Mississippi Railroad in the 1860s and not only was instrumental in getting work on the railroad started, but also helped to draw Jay Cooke into railroad development in Minnesota.
Photo by Charles A. Zimmerman
MHS

Symbolic construction began on February 15, 1870, near the very small settlement of Komoko, which disappeared within thirty years. Here, west of Thomson and the St. Louis River near the modern Highway 210 and the current highway maintenance yards in Carlton, was the level ground on which the railway could be built. It was just three weeks after raising the money, and the survey crews were still charting the actual route. As many as seventy-five people came from Duluth, Superior, Thomson, and Twin Lakes, most by sleigh, for the ceremony. The occasion opened with a prayer and Dr. Thomas P. Foster, editor of the *Duluth Minnesotian,* and others made speeches. A fire had been lit to melt the snow and the earth so that Colonel Joshua B. Culver, soon to be mayor of Duluth, could in a symbolic gesture fill the wheelbarrow, supplied by the contractor, and Colonel Hiram Hayes, city attorney of Superior, could wheel it away. Other dignitaries included the Reverends Mason Gallagher and George Slutor; General Ira Spaulding, the Chief Engineer for the Northern Pacific; General Thomas L. Rosser, a former Confederate cavalry officer and currently a civil engineer for the railroad; representatives from the Lake Superior & Mississippi Railroad; and sightseers from Thomson and Twin Lakes. It was recognized that this was the beginning of something very big and the cause for celebration. General Spaulding cabled Jay Cooke, "Ground broke on Northern Pacific Railroad today. One hundred men at work. Hurrah for the great enterprise! I have six parties of engineers in the field. Shall push the work vigorously." The wheelbarrow, pick, and shovel were sent to Cooke in Philadelphia as a memento of the great event.

The Beginnings of the Northern Pacific

Superior, Wisconsin
October 23, 1911

Mr. O.D. Wheeler
St. Paul, Minnesota

My dear Sir:

I have your inquiry of Oct. 16th regarding 'the time, the construction of the Northern Pacific Railroad was first begun.' The place was about 3/4th of a mile westerly from the Northern Pacific Junction, at a point a little northerly of the present track to Brainerd, in the dense wood. It was the site of a paper town, and then proposed by some exploiters, and a name was afterwards given to it—'Komoko.' An imaginary branch of the road was to start from Komoko and run to the Bay of Superior. The town and the branch were of course myths. It was in the month of February, 1870, that the work was begun there. Quite a crowd from Superior and from Duluth gathered on the spot that day, which may have been, I am not sure, the eighteenth. Speeches were made around the fire—a bon fire heaped with crackling limbs and burning with great alacrity. The deep snow melted and ran in torrents of water. The snow liquefied and so did the crowd. The earth thawed incidentally and so did all present for the occasion was one of hilarity and rejoicing for the start that was made.

A half dozen railroads might be building today, simultaneously, and not cause half the stir in the neighborhood as did that solitary start of the Northern Pacific, two and forty years ago.

The ground being well thawed, Col. J.B. Culver, a veteran of Chickamauga, and other fields, shoveled the wheelbarrow full of dirt, and I, myself, wheeled it to the dump—thereunto qualified, as having been a quartermaster of some of the forces at Chancellorsville, Gettysburg, Atlanta, Franklin, and Nashville, and many other minor occasions. I mention this only to say that soldiers of the Civil War had returned to civil duty, and were ready to shovel dirt, or trundle a wheelbarrow, and were not disposed to overturn the republic and hoist up an empire with their bayonets, in its place.

Gen. [Thomas L.] Rosser, a confederate cavalry officer of much renown, was at Komoko that day, booted but not spurred, wading in snow not gore. He was employed by the Northern Pacific in its Engineering Department. This signified the return of amity and fellowship as between North and South, which had been fighting three million or more of men all the way from the Potomac River to the Rio Grande.

Time has buried the historical spot referred to, and most of those then gathered on that day in February 1870. That was not the only memorable thing connected with the N.P at which I have attended. When [Josiah] Perham, the first President, was seeking its incorporation and land grant in the very early sixties, I sympathized at least, and somewhat cooperated with him in the city of Washington. The Act of Incorporation, etc. came in due time. When the surveys started from the Lake for the west in the early seventies, the engineers made my office head quarters at Superior, and such maps, acquaintance with the country, and some personal activity were at their disposal.

When the N.P. was reorganized under the laws of Wisconsin, I turned over to it the state charter, and a perfect organization under it, books, records and papers, which I had nursed and kept for many years, pertaining to the State Line R.R which was designed, among other things, to promote the construction of the branch to Superior, an idea which in one form or another had obsessed, as they say, my mind from an early period, not my mind alone, but that of a few others at Superior.

I have answered at some length your inquiry, but it may not be uninteresting to you as historical fact and verity.

Yours truly,
Hiram Hayes

Carlton County Vidette, 75th Anniversary Edition, February 24, 1964.

A number of trees were cut on that winter's day, but little of the real work other than surveying could be done in the winter season. Track crews for the Minnesota Division began their labors in the spring, satisfying the requirements for the federal land grant. Steel rails arrived from Detroit by ship in the summer and the work was facilitated by the first locomotive on the line, the small, saddle-tank *Minnetonka*, built by Smith & Porter of Pittsburgh, which is preserved in the Lake Superior Museum of Transportation and Industry in Duluth. The first spike was driven in early August (reputedly the same spike was also used to finish the transcontinental railroad thirteen years later in Gold Creek, Montana). By the end of work in November of 1870 the Northern Pacific reached Wright, at the western edge of Carlton County. The following season saw the first locomotive enter Moorhead on December 31, 1871, in a snow storm, and in 1873 the Northern Pacific reached the Missouri River, where the town of Bismarck was created.

The *Minnetonka*   Photo courtesy of Tim Johnson

The starting place of the Northern Pacific coincided with the tracks of the Lake Superior & Mississippi Railroad, building north from St. Paul and reaching across the St. Louis River to Thomson and eventually Duluth. The settlement there was called Komoko, which included some houses and a store that traded largely with local Indians. The first settler in Northern Pacific Junction is generally held to be a man named Gilbranson, who in 1870 built a cabin near where the Otter Creek flows into the St. Louis River. However, by that summer supplies and equipment were deposited on the level ground north of the Otter Creek midway between Komoko and the St. Louis. Tents, shanties, bunk houses, and eating facilities for the large work crews for both railroads were also set up and these formed the

Work crews excavating sand and gravel with a steam shovel at a pit on the Northern Pacific line near the site of the contemporary Black Bear Casino.
Photo courtesy of Dyhanne Lee

real origins of the settlement, a fairly rough and tumble frontier town. The men were paid $2.00 a day, but were charged $5.00 a week for room and board. A fire in Northern Pacific Junction in November, 1870, destroyed a drug store, two liquor stores, three saloons, and one general forwarding and commissioning store. This disaster did not alter the settlement's frontier character. The following year, 1871, Cooke, perhaps more concerned about the efficiency of his track crews than their morals, worried about reports that Northern Pacific Junction held over thirty saloons and several gambling dens, some being run by the same people who had plagued the building of the Union Pacific. A number of these entrepreneurs were taken to St. Paul in irons, tried, and sent to jail and passenger trains were ordered not to stop at Northern Pacific Junction in order to cut off liquor supplies, although this proved to be impractical. The trains had to service the settlement and the work crews had to be kept happy.

Happiness proved elusive for Jay Cooke and Company and the management of the Northern Pacific, however. Luck ran out. In 1873 Cooke's bank collapsed, unable to meet the financial obligations of the

Train depot at Northern Pacific Junction about 1884.

railroad. This led to the growing economic crisis in the United States, remembered as the Panic of 1873. The Northern Pacific went into receivership and was reorganized. New construction came to a halt and many plans had to be scrapped. For one thing, its lease and ownership relations with the Lake Superior & Mississippi Railroad were broken. The Lake Superior road also went into receivership and was reorganized as the St. Paul & Duluth Railroad in 1877. The Northern Pacific continued to use the jointly owned tracks from Northern Pacific Junction to Duluth, the shared depots, and it leased the tracks to St. Paul. (In 1900, in better times, the Northern Pacific bought the St. Paul & Duluth Railroad and acquired all of the valuable track of the latter.)

As economic conditions improved at the end of the 1870s both of the reorganized railroads began to expand and upgrade their services. In 1879 the St. Paul & Duluth built track north from Northern Pacific Junction to Knife Falls, which was later renamed Cloquet and which became one of the major sawmill towns in Minnesota. Logs from the extensive St. Louis River watershed in northeastern Minnesota could be floated downriver to Cloquet, without dealing with the problems created by Knife Falls itself and the Dalles of the St. Louis from Thomson to Fond du Lac. This guaranteed an enormous volume of rail traffic from Cloquet through Northern Pacific Junction. By 1882 the Northern Pacific was given very favorable terms (critics would say scandalous terms) to build tracks into Superior, Wisconsin, from Northern Pacific Junction southwest through Wrenshall and over the height of land between the St. Louis River and the Nemadji River into Superior. This was the first rail line into Superior, and in 1884 the line was also extended to Ashland, Wisconsin. In addition to giving Superior access by railroad, beginning in 1911 this line allowed the Northern Pacific to carry iron ore from

Saint Paul & Duluth Short Line train in 1893 crossing the St. Louis River at Thomson and heading to Carlton from Duluth.

the Cuyuna range into its two newly constructed docks in Allouez, south of Superior. In 1886 the St. Paul & Duluth built new tracks east from Thomson and around the escarpment of the Duluth hills into West Duluth Junction—the "Duluth Short Line"—reducing the route by two and a half miles and improving the grade of the original track along the St. Louis River valley from 103 feet per mile to 52 feet per mile. (This new route eventually rendered the original Lake Superior & Mississippi track along the St. Louis River valley obsolete. A fire destroyed the longest wooden trestle in 1894, and the Fond du Lac line was taken out of use in 1898.) By the early twentieth century the traffic in the Northern Pacific's yards at Rice's Point in Duluth was so great that to relieve the congestion, the Carlton yards (which held 2.3 miles of track in 57 acres) and shops, which were already extensive, were expanded in 1912. The town could take pleasure in the revived success of the Northern Pacific Railroad and its completion as a transcontinental railway in 1883. The village council voted $50 to celebrate the September visit of the company's new president, Henry Villard, on his way west to drive the last spike to complete the northern rail system.

The next decade saw two new railroads enter Carlton. James J. Hill was able to acquire the strug-

Great Northern ore train going through Carlton, up bound, about 1904.

The Northern Pacific yards in Carlton, seen in 1928 from the Great Northern switch tower. The identification key is as follows: 1) Northern Pacific 3rd Subdivision, Duluth to St. Paul (former Lake Superior & Mississippi Railroad); 14) switch lead to coal dock and east yard; 15) switch lead to Northern Pacific 2nd Subdivision, to Superior; 16) Northern Pacific 2nd Subdivision, Carlton to Staples; 18) Northern Pacific 2nd Subdivision, Carlton to Superior; 19) Eastbound 2nd Subdivision signal stand; 20) yard lead Northern Pacific 2nd Subdivision to yard; 21) Northern Pacific coal dock track; 22) yard lead from yard to 3rd Subdivision (Duluth) and 7th Subdivision (Cloquet); 25) rip track (car repair track); 35) Great Northern westbound main track (Superior to Range and Grand Rapids); 36) Great Northern eastbound main track (Grand Rapids and Range to Superior); A) Village of Carlton road crossing; B) Northern Pacific and Milwaukee Railroads Depot; C) Signal stand, eastbound Northern Pacific yard and 3rd Subdivision to Duluth and Cloquet (also Northern Pacific wye); D) trainmen's shack; E) rail crossing for the Great Northern eastbound and Northern Pacific 3rd Subdivision; F) rail crossing for Great Northern westbound and Northern Pacific 3rd Subdivision; G) Northern Pacific coal dock; J) Great Northern signal maintainers shack; K) Minnesota State Highway 61 bridge; L) Great Northern eastbound home signal; M) Northern Pacific 3rd Subdivision platform; O) yard switch and derail; P) Northern Pacific puzzle switches 2nd and 3rd Subdivisions operated from the Great Northern tower; R) Great Northern interlocking fuse boxes; S) Great Northern interlocking trunklines (the switch between R and S in the lower right corner is for the west leg of the wye to Cloquet).
Photo from the collection of Wayne C. Olson courtesy of Tim Johnson

gling Duluth & Winnipeg Railway in 1896, after it went into receivership following the Panic of 1893, and integrate it into the Great Northern Railroad in 1898. This railroad, once it was extended farther west, enabled Hill's Great Northern Railroad to connect Duluth with his main line, also a transcontinental since 1893, at Grand Forks, North Dakota. He abandoned the existing track from Cloquet to Duluth and constructed new track from Cloquet though Carlton and southeast past Wrenshall to State Line and Boylston in 1898, entering Superior where the Great Northern already had rail yards. Hill also acquired a logging railroad and its properties north of Swan River which contained the richest iron ore deposits of the Mesabi range. The result was that vast numbers of Great Northern ore trains bound for the docks at Allouez, Wisconsin, passed though Carlton on double track. The last railroad to enter Carlton was the Chicago,

Milwaukee & St. Paul. After threatening to build its own tracks into Duluth, the "Milwaukee Road" negotiated an arrangement with the Northern Pacific in 1900 to share the track and facilities of their lines from St. Paul to Duluth through Carlton. By 1900 the St. Paul & Duluth Railroad was also finally acquired by the Northern Pacific and fully integrated into its system. The result was that as the twentieth century opened Carlton was a major junction for three of America's great railroads—the Northern Pacific, the Great Northern, and the Milwaukee Road.

All of this railroad building and activity made Northern Pacific Junction a major railroad hub. By the end of the 1880s railroad tracks entered the town from five different directions: west from the Northern Pacific main line, southwest from the Twin Cities, southeast from Superior, east from Thomson and Duluth, and north from Cloquet and beyond. In 1891, on the St. Paul & Duluth Railroad line alone, 58 trains went through Carlton per day, including six regular passenger trains and two to Cloquet. The Northern Pacific ran six regular passenger trains and twenty-six freight trains with "monster mogul engines." Carlton (Northern Pacific Junction) had in fact become the transportation and commercial hub that visionaries had imagined would be the future of Thomson. However, unlike Thomson which provided access only east to Duluth, Carlton was located sufficiently beyond the St. Louis River to give access to all four points of the compass—east and west, north and south. It was Carlton's distinction to be the site of the beginning of the Northern Pacific, but it was Carlton's good fortune to be located on a sufficient plateau above the St. Louis River to make it a pivotal railroad center.

After having made a success of the St. Paul & Pacific Railroad (reorganized into the Great Northern), James J. Hill expanded his operations north to Superior. In the 1890s he bought the Duluth & Winnipeg Railroad that extended northwest up the St. Louis River from Cloquet and a logging railroad and cut-over timberlands on the Mesabi Range. Able to bring vast trainloads of iron ore down from the Range, Hill built tracks to his facilities in Superior, bringing double track through Carlton in 1898 in the process.
Photo - MHS, October 5, 1911

A summer Sunday in Carlton in 1885, and an opportunity for an outing. The ladies with long skirts, hats, and bouquets, the gents with hats and ties, and a Saint Paul & Duluth sidecar for convenience.

The Future of the Northern Pacific

"There is no doubt that this line of road [the Northern Pacific] will do an immense amount of business. Such is the estimations in which it is held by the moneyed men of Philadelphia, that Mr. Jay Cooke obtained the entire amount of money necessary to construct it in four days! The bonds, I believe, were not put upon the market in the usual manner, by advertising, but were taken at once by men who wanted them for investment."

Charles Carleton Coffin, *The Seat of Empire* (Boston: Fields, Osgood & Co., 1870), pp. 159-60.

"Almost in the centre of the Dalles I passed the spot where the Northern Pacific Railroad had on that day turned its first sod, commencing its long course across the continent. This Northern Pacific Railroad is destined to play a great part in the future history of the United States; it is the second great link which is to bind together the Atlantic and Pacific States (before twenty years there will be many others)."

William Francis Butler, *The Great Lone Land: A Narrative of Travel and Adventure in the North West of America* (Edmonton: M.G. Hurtig, Ltd., 1968 [first published, 1872]), p. 68.

Sources:

Carroll, Francis M. *Crossroads in Time: A History of Carlton County, Minnesota.* Cloquet: Carlton County Historical Society, 1987.

Harnsberger, John L. *Jay Cooke and Minnesota: The Formative Years of the Northern Pacific Railroad, 1868-1873.* New York: Arno Press, 1981.

King, Frank A. "Railroads at the Head of the Lakes," in Ryck Lydecker and Lawrence Sommer (eds.), *Duluth, Sketches of the Past: A Bicentennial Collection.* Duluth: American Revolutionary Bicentennial Commission, 1976.

Lubetkin, M. John. "'Twenty-Six Feet and No Bottom': Surveying and Constructing the Northern Pacific Railroad," *Minnesota History*, vol. 60, no. 1 (Spring, 2006).

Oberholtzer, Ellis Paxson. *Jay Cooke: Financier of the Civil War.* New York: Augustus M. Kelly, 1968, Vol. II.

Prosser, Richard S. *Rails to the North Star: One Hundred Years of Railroad Evolution in Minnesota.* Minneapolis: Dillon Press, 1966.

"Gandy dancers!" Nicholson's section crew tamping railroad tracks in the Carlton yard. The jack can be seen in place to level the track to the correct position. The crew stands with their shovels, ready to "tamp" the ballast under the ties to hold the track in the proper position. The storefronts in the town can be seen behind the men.

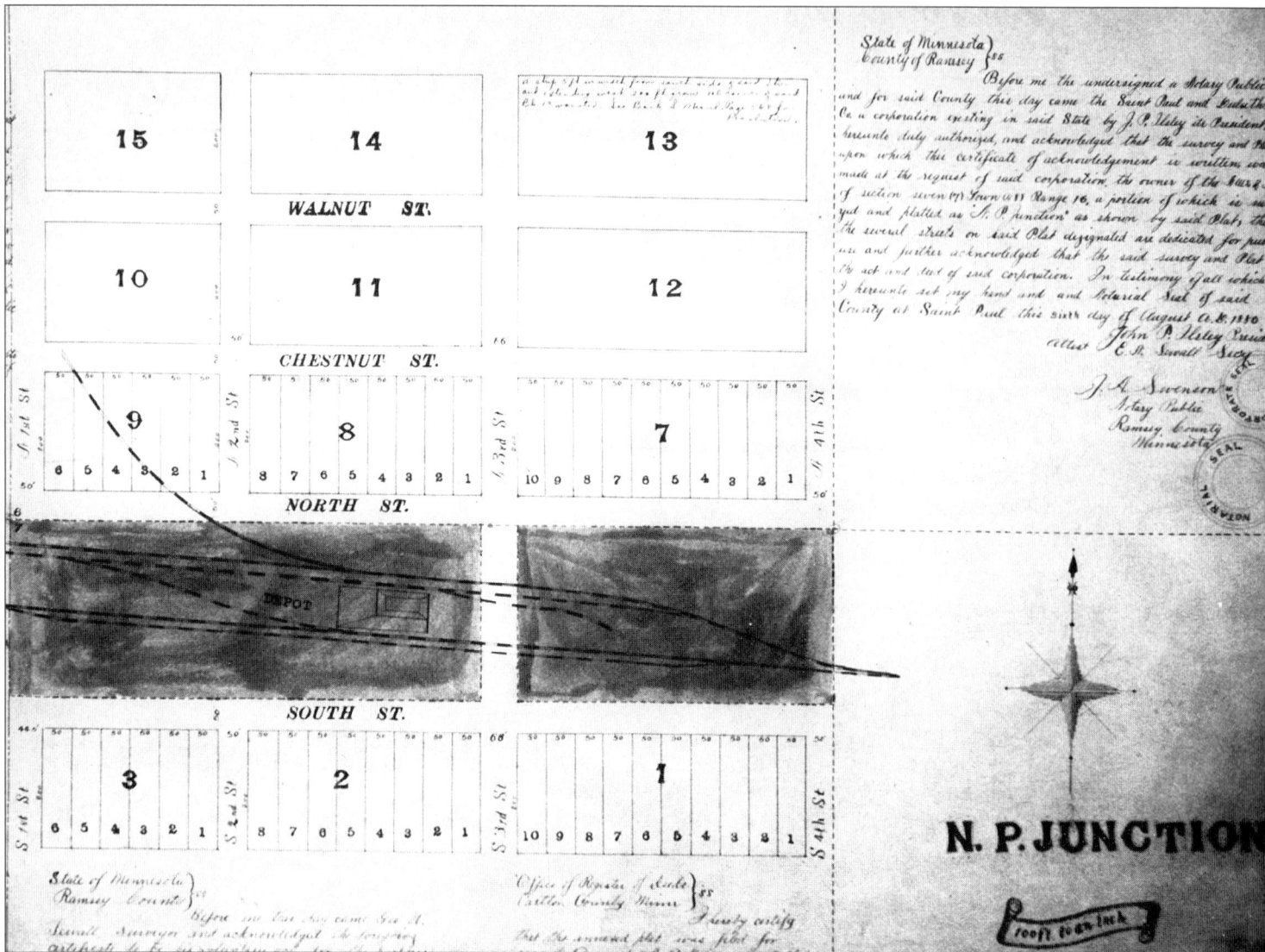

This 1880 map of Northern Pacific Junction shows the recognizable layout of the town streets. The original depot was placed well east of its subsequent location. The map shows the east leg of the wye, built in 1879, to what became Cloquet, but the southern track to Superior, Wisconsin, would not be constructed until 1882.
Map courtesy of Carlton County Abstract & Title Company

A spring day in Carlton in the 1890s. People are still in their winter coats and hats, but the snow has melted off the boardwalk and even parts of the street.

CHAPTER 3

A Lumber Town

In the nineteenth century the building of a railroad stimulated what economists call the "multiplier effect" in the surrounding region. Nowhere was this more true than in Carlton County and specifically in Northern Pacific Junction. This is particularly clear in the population statistics. The first census in the county was taken in 1860 and registered 51 white settlers. Ten years later, as the railroads were being built, the total population was only 286, of which 163 lived in Thomson where the railroad building was most complete, and only 27 were listed in "Railroad Junction" as it was called in the Census, or Northern Pacific Junction, where railroad building was just beginning. By 1880 the population of the county had jumped to 1,230, of which 298 were listed in Twin Lakes township and most of those were in Northern Pacific Junction. By 1890, after the completion of much of the rail network, Carlton County reached 5,272, and the town of Carlton had reached a significant figure of 612. While all of the settlements along the railroad and the newly opened farmland had prospered and expanded, Cloquet was the greatest beneficiary. Thanks to the combination of the railroad, providing extensive markets through Northern Pacific Junction, and the St. Louis River and the pinelands in its watershed, clear of obstruction above Knife Falls, the lumber industry had swelled its population to 2,530. (And it would continue to grow to upwards of 8,500 to 9,000 on the eve of the 1918 fire.)

The railroads had a particularly symbiotic relationship with the lumber industry because railroads were both major users of wood in various forms and facilitators of the marketing of forest products. Railroad ties were consumed in vast quantities (between 2,200 and 3,500 per mile, and they had to replaced regularly), large timbers were used for trestles and station platforms (not to mention grain elevators and ore docks that were to come later), finished lumber for stations and sheds, and, until late in the 19th century, huge amounts of firewood to drive the engines. Furthermore, as the railroads gave access to farms and towns a steady market for lumber was created to build houses, barns, and urban facilities. Through the land grants given to the railroads these companies possessed extensive timberlands which typically they sold to lumbermen to earn revenue. Finally, the railroads carried a large proportion of the lumber products from the sawmills to market (sawmills in Duluth, other Great Lakes ports, and various towns along the Mississippi River could also ship lumber to market by water transportation). As early as 1872 the Lake Superior & Mississippi Railroad was carrying almost twenty-two million board feet of lumber south to St. Paul.

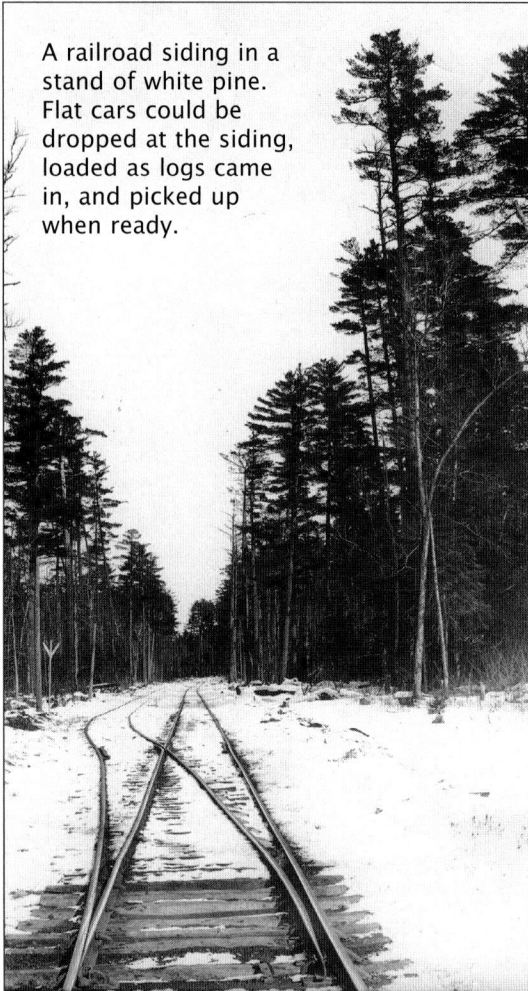

A railroad siding in a stand of white pine. Flat cars could be dropped at the siding, loaded as logs came in, and picked up when ready.

As for Carlton County, it was richly endowed with the choice trees of the lumber industry—eastern white pine. By some accounts the county's production of 94,000 board feet of white pine per acre was a record, when 25,000 feet was considered good and 10,000 feet was still profitable. Well before 1870 and Northern Pacific Junction, logging operations had been working their way up from Stillwater and the St. Croix River into the Kettle River and its tributaries in the southwestern part of the county. Similarly, lumbermen in Superior and Duluth had sent crews into both the lower St. Louis River and more specifically the Nemadji River in the southeastern part of the county. In the 1890s the Mitchell and McClure Company of Duluth extended a logging railroad into the Nemadji River valley, necessitating an enormous trestle that was nearly 750 feet long and over 100 feet above the river. With the building of the Lake Superior & Mississippi Railroad to Thomson lumbermen could tap new forests above the Dalles of the St. Louis. The first to take advantage of this opportunity was Charles Usterhouse who built a sawmill at Thomson in 1870. Andreas M. Miller moved his larger sawmill from Duluth to Thomson the following year. Miller first brought logs down the Midway River and later built a logging railroad to reach timber beyond that stream. Miller made a fortune and closed down his operations in 1891. For a time, Thomson had three sawmills.

Captain James M. Paine brought the lumber industry into Northern Pacific Junction. Paine came from Maine and served in two Minnesota regiments in the Civil War, distinguishing himself during the Sioux Uprising of 1862. In the late 1860s he started a sawmill in Oneota and found a ready market in providing lumber for the Lake Superior & Mississippi Railroad, of which his uncle, Parker Paine, was a director. With the completion of

An early photograph of the Paine Lumber Company yard, looking east from Carlton. The large American type locomotive, "Chip," is straight ahead. Clearly visible is the large sawmill and the bull chain to draw the logs up from the millpond to the saws on the second floor. The office and general store is to the right.

that railroad and the starting of the Northern Pacific, Paine moved his mill to Northern Pacific Junction in 1870 in partnership with Eugene M. Wilson and William W. McNair. The operations were located on the north bank of Otter Creek, on the eastern edge of the settlement. From this position Paine was able to cut timber in the Otter Creek valley nearly as far west as Big Lake and continue to serve his railroad customers. In 1875 the mill burned down and Paine rebuilt an expanded facility after having bought out his partners.

When the readily accessible pinelands along Otter Creek were exhausted by 1886, Paine built a logging railroad south of Northern Pacific Junction in Silver Brook and Twin Lakes townships to continue cutting white pine. This was the first logging railroad in Minnesota, although others had been developed further east. It was expensive, costing $60,000,

The J.M. Paine and Company sawmill, as seen from the rocks in Carlton. The bull chain, used to draw the logs from the millpond up to the saws on the second floor, can be seen extending down from the structure. The building to the left was the shop and dressed lumber shed; the facility in the center was the planer. Stacks of cut lumber can be seen drying on the right.

but it paid off. Freed from river transportation, Paine could keep his sawmill running twelve months a year, and by the end of the decade was producing 12,000,000 board feet of lumber a year, 4,000,000 feet of lath, and 4,000,000 feet of shingles. Initially working one engine and nine cars, Paine's railroad grew to three engines and twenty-five cars. The first engine was a thirty-year old, pre-Civil War, high wheeled, 4-4-0, American type locomotive called "Chip," the second was one of the four original Northern Pacific saddle tank, 0-4-0, Porter locomotives nicknamed "Avis," and the third was a new twenty-eight ton Shay, geared, logging locomotive, called "Lizzie." These engines pulled as many as three train loads of logs a day into the Paine yards in Carlton.

A train at Coryell, a camp south of Carlton, loaded with logs for the Paine sawmill. The locomotive, "Lizzie," was a Shay logging engine, designed to operate slowly over uneven roadbeds. Rather than pistons turning large driving wheels in a pounding motion, these pistons turned a geared shaft that was connected to smaller drive wheels, producing a motion less likely to propel the engine off the tracks. The engineer was Chris Bandle, Bill Sheils is in the foreground, and Jack Haubner and "Long Jack" Anderson are on the logs.

Captain Paine had a large number of people working for him at the sawmill, perhaps as many as forty or fifty, and also a substantial number of loggers working in camps in the woods, anywhere from thirty to sixty men in each camp and possibly several camps a year. Maurice Haubner has estimated that there may have been over a thousand lumberjacks working in the Carlton area. The lumberjacks in the camps cut the trees and, using oxen drawn "go devils," skidded the logs, often between two to four feet in diameter, to either the stream bank or the railroad siding. Throughout much of the nineteenth century the logs would be driven downstream to the sawmills when the ice went out in the spring. With the logging railroad the logs could be delivered to the sawmill in winter or summer, making the lumber

Sleighs full of logs are shown being delivered to a landing on the South Fork of the Nemadji River. The logs would be piled here during the winter and pushed into the river when the ice went out in the spring. They would then be floated, or run, down the river to sawmills in Superior or the Duluth Harbor. William Sheils is shown in front.

business less of a seasonal operation. In addition to the lumberjacks, all sorts of skilled people were required in the camps: teamsters to drive the horses, blacksmiths to make equipment and shoe the horses, cooks to feed the men, filers to keep the saws sharp, and bookkeepers to see that the men got paid and the logs were accounted for. Some of the Carlton names that were attached to the Paine operations were: Alex Beattie, Alex McFarland, Sam Clark, Tom McCausland, S.A. Carlson, and James Dunphy. The founding of a second company, the Carlton Lumber Company, was undertaken in 1882, with Frederick W. Paine as one of the directors. The Paine family and their operations had a profound influence on the growth of Northern Pacific Junction and the early Carlton.

The Lumber Industry in Carlton County

"White pine is found in every county in Minnesota east of the Mississippi from Minneapolis to Canada. ... Itasca, St. Louis, Mille Lacs, Kanabec, Pine, Aitkin, Beltrami, Cass, and Carlton counties had especially fine stands, but Carlton County was its favored abode. That county was originally more heavily timbered with white pine than any other county in the state. There is authentic evidence of one acre of white pine in Carlton County which yielded, by actual measurement, 94,000 feet of lumber. That was a record."

Agnes Larson. *History of the White Pine Industry in Minnesota*. New York: Arno Press, 1972 [first published, 1949].

Captain James M. Paine

James M. Paine was born at North Anson, Maine, in 1834. As a young man he moved to Boston and in the mid-1850s followed his uncle, Parker Paine, to Minnesota where he entered the lumber business. Paine served in a Minnesota regiment in the Civil War and participated as an officer on the staff of General Alfred Sully's command during the Sioux Uprising of 1862 and its aftermath. Captain Paine was mentioned for gallantry during General Sully's cavalry expedition into the Dakota Territory in 1864 and 1865. After the war Paine returned to the lumber business, opening a sawmill in Oneota in Duluth. He supplied lumber to the Lake Superior & Mississippi Railroad, in which his uncle, Parker Paine, was a director. In 1870 Paine bought the mill in partnership with Eugene M. Wilson and William W. McNair and moved it to the new Northern Pacific Junction. There he supplied lumber to

Captain James M. Paine in the uniform of a Civil War officer. As a former Union Army officer and a mill owner Paine was a figure of some substance in the first thirty years of Carlton's history. Photo by Nowack & Palmer - MHS

the Northern Pacific Railroad, specializing in the beams used in building trestles and bridges. When the mill burned down in 1875, Paine bought out his partners and formed J.M. Paine and Company. Paine's mill was located on the north bank of Otter Creek east of the settlement. Otter Creek had quite an extensive watershed west of the settlement, the north branch reaching almost to Big Lake and Little Otter Creek extending beyond Iverson to the south. When the trees in close proximity to Otter Creek were nearly all cut, Paine began to build a logging railroad southeast into Silver Brook Township in order to cut timber that could not be floated to the mill by any stream. By expanding to three locomotives and at least twenty-five cars, Paine was able to cut trees in Twin Lakes Township and to keep his logging operations and sawmill going all year long. By the mid-1890s the mill produced about twenty million board feet of lumber per year and the company employed about one hundred men. The company also maintained a general store and a grain elevator, as well as selling land from its extensive holdings. Paine had several residences, including Carlton and Chub Lake, where he also had a steam launch. Captain Paine died in March, 1900, on his way back from spending the winter in Florida.

Captain Paine was survived by his wife, Ellen Adele Elkins, who continued to make her home in Carlton for part of every year, and four grown children. Their son, Asa Paine, worked in the lumber business, the Carlton County Bank, real estate, and other enterprises; after some financial reverses he went to Vancouver, British Columbia, to recoup his fortunes and he died there in 1916. The three daughters lived variously in Carlton and elsewhere: Elizabeth, who married Frederic Allen Williams of Boston; Ellen Adele, known as "Lovey," who married Jean Maurice Blandin, a companion of the Legion of Honor from Dijon France, and who later as a widow lived in New York; and Cordelia. Ms. Cordelia Ayer Paine was educated at Stetson University, Rollins College, and the University of Minnesota. She studied music in Boston, Berlin, and Paris, had a career as a concert pianist in New York, and composed over 200 works. She also built a new house, "Stonecroft," for her mother in Carlton, managed the Paine estate, founded the Carlton area Red Cross, and, with her sister, Mme. Blandin, helped to start the Carlton Library. During World War I she served overseas with the YMCA and brought wounded French soldiers to the United States. She was treasurer of the Congress of States, a director of the Edgar Allen Poe Society, a founder of the National Arts Council, co-chairman of the Dickens-Irving American Fellowship, a life member of the Colonial Order of the Crown, historian of the Daughters of the American Revolution, and a member of the Daughters of the Founders and Patriots of America. She lived out her days in the Home of the Association for the Relief of Respectable Aged Indigent Females in New York and died in 1960.

Captain Paine also brought to Carlton his cousin, Mark Paine, who assisted him in the lumber business and who served as the first president of the village council of Northern Pacific Junction. Still another Paine connection was Frederick W. Paine who formed the briefly functioning Carlton Lumber Company.

Carlton County Vidette, August 25, 1884, March 23 and 24, 1900, and March 25, 1940.
Carlton County Historical Society records.

The Sauntry-Cain Company took over the J.M. Paine and Company after Captain Paine died in March of 1900. William Sauntry and W. Martin Cain were lumbermen with roots in Ireland, New Brunswick, and Stillwater, Minnesota. Sauntry had formed partnerships with several lumbermen in the St. Croix and by 1894 had joined with Martin Cain to begin logging operations in the tributaries of the Kettle River in Carlton County. The Sauntry-Cain Company sent a substantial amount of logs down the Kettle River to Stillwater, also using logging railroads to extend their operations, but in the course of the 1890s, with their main office in Barnum, they built sawmills at Blackhoof, Sandy Lake, Atkinson, and the village of Sauntry, north of Atkinson. The Sauntry-Cain Company specialized in the highest quality white pine lumber; the beams visible today in the ceiling of the Union Depot in Duluth are an example from the Sauntry-Cain operations at Sandy Lake. When they took over the Paine mill in Carlton they introduced many improvements, including the largest double band saw in the United States at the time, a new planing mill, electrification, and telephones. Indeed, Martin Cain developed and patented a release mechanism that allowed heavy logs to be off-loaded from railway cars without danger to the workmen. Their operations pushed further into Silver Brook and Twin Lakes townships, using horse drawn sleighs with huge loads of logs over iced roads in order to extend the reach of the logging railroad. The operations out of Carlton employed as many as seven hundred twenty-four men. Through his connections with the Weyerhaeuser interests, William Sauntry was able also to become a one-fifth shareholder in the Superior Timber Company, incorporated in August 1901. The purpose of this company was

A cookhouse in a Sauntry-Cain Company lumber camp. Women were often employed as cooks in the Sauntry-Cain camps, helping to create a more home-like atmosphere. The presence of the young boy and the young man with his rifle suggest this occasion is probably a Sunday.

to collect and cut into finished lumber the logs owned by Weyerhaeuser and various other allied interests in northern Wisconsin. Several Duluth and Superior sawmills were selected to cut the logs, but in fact the Carlton mills cut the largest proportion of them. A disastrous fire destroyed the new $10,000 planing mill in February 1903, although the facility was quickly rebuilt. The Sauntry-Cain operation was kept running at full capacity until 1906, when it was dismantled and shipped to Oregon to be reassembled and operated by Martin Cain's younger brother. Sauntry-Cain took the Carlton lumber business into the twentieth century.

Much of the forest history of Minnesota can be seen in the operations of these two companies. The winter lumber camps, with spring log drives down the rivers to other mills, were followed by the development of larger and larger local sawmill operations. The "State of Maine" lumber camps built close to the streams, with old-fashioned "shotgun" bunks, were succeeded by New Brunswick-Irish camps, which were more elaborate, better fed, and with women and families working and visiting. Sawmill equipment and facilities were steadily upgraded, substantially increasing the volume of board feet cut per year, and this was further augmented by the logging railroads that could bring in timber all year long. Carlton did not become the permanent forest industry center that Cloquet did, but for thirty-five years it was a major part of the Minnesota white pine lumber industry.

William Martin Cain

William Martin Cain
Photo courtesy of the Sauntry-Cain Company

W. Martin Cain was born on April 12, 1858, in Old Northesk, New Brunswick, where he worked in the lumber business as a youth. At age 18 he moved to Michigan and later to Wisconsin and in 1879 came to Stillwater, Minnesota, where in 1884 he and his brother, John Stewart Cain, united with George W. Robinson, also a New Brunswicker, to form Robinson-Cain Company which supplied logs to William Sauntry. In 1888 Martin Cain joined William and Joseph Sauntry, two other New Brunswickers who ran extensive logging operations out of Stillwater, to create the Sauntry-Cain Company. This company undertook extensive logging operations in the St. Croix and Kettle River valleys. In 1893 they started a sawmill at Blackhoof under Cain's management that produced about 40,000 board feet per day. By the end of the 1890s the Sauntry-Cain Company had its main office and company store in Barnum, a sales office in Stillwater, sawmills in Sandy Lake, Carlton, and Atkinson, and a railroad siding at "Sauntry," a small village on the St. Paul & Duluth (Northern Pacific) line north of Atkinson.

The security force at a Sauntry-Cain lumber camp in the mid-1890s. Guards were often needed to prevent theft of logs.

Photo - MHS

After Captain James M. Paine's death in 1900, Sauntry-Cain bought the sawmill at Carlton from the Paine estate, which they were able to expand, improve, and operate for several years. Sauntry-Cain Company employed over seven hundred men and in 1901 produced twenty-two million board feet of white pine lumber. After closing the sawmill in 1906, Martin Cain remained in Carlton, managing the contract cutting of timber in Carlton, St. Louis, and Itasca counties and undertaking both road building and railroad construction. A "Progressive" Republican in political sympathy, he even supported Theodore Roosevelt in 1912 when "T.R." broke with the Grand Old Party and ran for president as a "Bull Moose" candidate. Cain was sufficiently concerned about public affairs to serve as a member of the board of county commissioners for eight years and became president of the Carlton village council in 1905. Cain, together with Henry Oldenburg, arranged for the athletic park near the school, and he saw to it that the swampy land was drained, filled, and leveled to make excellent playing fields.

Martin Cain married Zelpha Tozer, a member of a Stillwater lumber family, in 1883 and they had four children: Maud M., who married James A. Gillespie of Carlton; George S., who died early; William D., who lived in Duluth; and Warren A., who lived in Carlton. His first wife died in Barnum 1894 and was buried in Stillwater. In 1896 Cain married Hannah Johnson of Barnum and they had six children: Gladys and John, who died in infancy; Merton E., who served as Postmaster in Carlton; A. Ralph, of Carlton; Grace E., who married J. Whitney Carr of Seward, Nebraska; and Willard M., of Cloquet. Cain died in his home on Third Street on June 25, 1932. He was given a large funeral at the Paine Presbyterian Church and was buried in Barnum.

Anniversary Edition of the Carlton County Vidette, January 11, 1908.
Carlton County Vidette, June 30, 1932.

Sources:

Haubner, Maurice H. *Pillars of Society*. Privately printed, 1983. Pp. 12-13.

King, Frank A. *Minnesota Logging Railroads: A Pictorial History of the Era When White Pine and Logging Railroads Reigned Supreme*. San Marino: Golden West Books, 1981.

Larson, Agnes. *History of the White Pine Industry in Minnesota*. New York: Arno Press, 1972 [first published, 1949].

Ryan, J.C. "The Duluth Lumber Industry," in Ryck Lydecker and Lawrence Sommer (eds.). *Duluth, Sketches of the Past: A Bicentennial History*. Duluth: American Revolution Bicentennial Commission, 1976.

Superior Timber Company Papers, P 475, Minnesota Historical Society Collection.

Twining, Charles E. "The Lumbering Frontier," in Susan L. Flader (ed.). *The Great Lakes Forest: An Environmental and Social History*. Minneapolis: University of Minnesota Press, 1983.

A hot lunch was served to the lumberjacks in the woods if they were over a mile from the camp. The "cookee," or assistant cook, would bring hot bread, meat and vegetables, pie, and coffee on a sled, or "swing-dingle," that was padded with blankets to keep the meals hot. Alex Prevost, standing at left, had just brought dinner out in the sled.

Margaret Oldenburg and Della Sheils as two young lumberjacks in 1904.
Photo courtesy of Barb Schmidt

Timber cruisers went into the woods ahead of the lumberjacks, identified and marked the sections to be cut, and assessed the value of the timber. Theirs was an important and well paying job, but it was a solitary existence. Ali Albertson and William Sheils are shown here in front of their tent. They obviously cook for themselves, and the reflector oven to the right suggests that they knew what they were doing.

Ed Sheils in 1885 with his well-known six oxen team hitched to a sleigh loaded with logs. Sheils was hauling logs for Andreas M. Miller of Thomson in the Midway River valley.

After a tree had been cut, the branches were removed and it was usually cut into sixteen-foot logs. These logs would then be skidded to a loading area by a team of horses.

Photo by Nelson Freeman

Cooks posing in the cookhouse in one of the early lumber camps. Meals in lumber camps had to be good or the lumberjacks would quit. Pea soup and ham, beans and pork, roast beef, potatoes and gravy, stewed prunes, apple pie, coffee and tea, tended to be the favorites. This kitchen is spacious and appears well equipped.

Photo by Nelson Freeman

This festively clad band helped to celebrate the 4th of July in Carlton in 1909. They are identified as McFarland, Fisher, H. Freeman, H. Masney, T. Pearson, H. Olson, F. Cooper, O. Nicholson, H. Karnowski, G. Cain, L. Flynn.

Photo courtesy of Darold Powers

CHAPTER 4

A Railroad Town

Between the railways, which built shops, engine houses, and switch yards, and the lumber business, with sawmills, railroads, yards, and camps, Northern Pacific Junction began to attract a permanent population, as well as commerce and services. In 1881 the St. Paul & Duluth Railroad built a new water tank, a new freight warehouse, expanded the engine house to hold two engines, and drafted plans to rebuild the bridge over the St. Louis River, which was jointly owned with the Northern Pacific Railroad. A decade later the two railroads felt the need to upgrade the line between Thomson and Fond du Lac, and the Short Line Railroad from Thomson to Duluth, which suffered from inferior construction and needed extensive maintenance. On April 2, 1897, the Carlton depot, which was shared by both railroads, was destroyed by fire. Both the ticket agent and the waiting room were temporarily placed in nearby buildings while plans were considered for a new depot. One proposal was to move an existing structure from Smithville, in Duluth, to Carlton. Henry C. Oldenburg wrote to the Assistant General Manager of the St. Paul & Duluth urging him to build a new depot out of the slate bricks made in the new brick plant in Thomson. He was sent a polite reply, but the depot built was of wood frame construction. In 1896 James J. Hill's Great Northern Railroad acquired the Duluth & Winnipeg Railway, which had tracks from Duluth to Cloquet and proceeded up the St. Louis River and as far west as Swan River. Hill abandoned the tracks east of Cloquet going to Duluth, and in 1898 built a new right-of-way through Carlton southeast to State Line and Boylston to connect with his Great Northern yards and facilities in Superior. To do this Hill had to negotiate the right to cross the tracks of the two other railroads and to use the depot and freight facilities in Carlton. All of this meant a lot of construction was undertaken in the Carlton yards in the 1890s.

The depot in Carlton was owned and operated by the Northern Pacific Railroad, but from the 1890s it rented services to the Great Northern Railroad on a very profitable basis. The American Railway Express (parcel) service and the Western Union Telegraph (message) service were also located in the depot, making it a very vital part of the community.
Photo courtesy of Dyhanne Lee

Carlton seemed poised on the edge of still greater railroad development. The opening up of the western prairie wheat land, as well as the new iron ore mining on the

Mesabi and Cuyuna ranges, channeled increased numbers of both Northern Pacific and Great Northern trains through Carlton to Duluth and Superior in the early twentieth century. Not even regular maintenance and track improvement could smooth out all of the problems that this heavy traffic created. By early 1912 the Northern Pacific management concluded that the greatest congestion the railroad experienced was between Duluth and St. Paul and Duluth and Staples. The solution was to build new larger terminal facilities in Carlton. Thus, during the summer of 1913 bids were accepted for the construction of a large twenty-four stall brick roundhouse, a 100 foot turntable, a brick machine shop, a brick boiler house, a brick store house, a three track coal dock, two 100,000 gallon water tanks, various other buildings and sheds, and expanded switching yards. The *Carlton County Vidette* greeted the news of these plans with enthusiasm, as the railroad was buying land for its new yards, and commented on how many people the new terminal would employ. By early April the Northern Pacific had forty men working on the expansion of the yards. However, on June 27, 1913, the *Vidette* reported that "All

Looking west from 3rd Street at the Northern Pacific Railroad engine house, July 1928. Key - B) signal maintenance car and tool house, D) engine men's bunk house, E) four stall engine house, F) N.P. lineman car and tool house, L) N.P. sand house.
Photo from the collection of Wayne C. Olsen,
courtesy of Tim Johnson

operations of the Northern Pacific Railroad Company in the way of trackage and roundhouse machine shed and other buildings at this point have ceased." The contractor was told to pack up his equipment and men and move them out. The explanation was that the United States Supreme Court decision on the Minnesota freight rate case resulted in a lowering of the rate throughout the state, and the result was that the Northern Pacific was pulling back on numerous expansion projects. In the autumn the Northern Pacific ran a large advertisement in the *Vidette* assuring people that, "One of the great pieces of work which we will undertake this Spring will be the enlargement of the track facilities of the terminal yards at Carlton." In the end, only the track facilities were expanded. The twenty-four stall roundhouse and the other terminal shops and buildings were never put in place. The railroad had reached its high water mark in Carlton.

Train Wrecks

Although railroads were among the most ingenious inventions of the nineteenth century, they were susceptible to accidents. The first recorded railroad accident in Carlton County took place on the Lake Superior & Mississippi line between Carlton and Moose Lake in late November, 1870, when a broken axle on a rail car carrying sugar and molasses resulted in a derailment and pile-up. One can only imagine the scenes. Personal injuries were horrendous, brakemen being particularly vulnerable while working between the cars or walking along their tops while the train was moving at full speed. Many people were maimed or killed by train accidents. A constant danger was collision, particularly when single tracks were used by trains going in different directions and signals systems were imperfect. Derailments occurred frequently and might have either minor or major consequences.

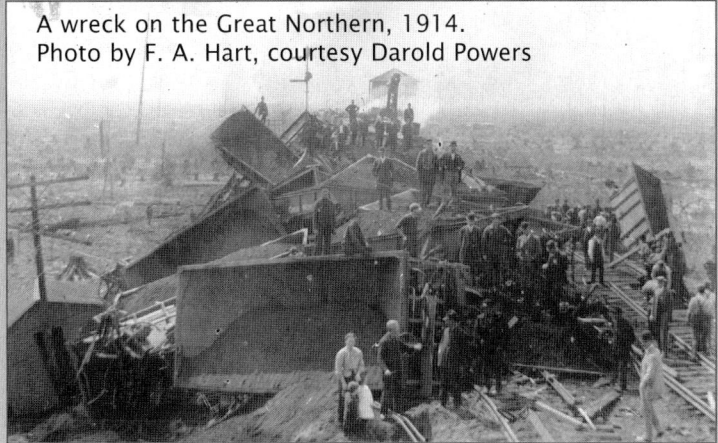

A wreck on the Great Northern, 1914.
Photo by F. A. Hart, courtesy Darold Powers

Often the results of train wrecks were spectacular and provided a somewhat grim form of entertainment. People would be drawn to see the often twisted and shattered engine and cars, and to watch the skillful and complicated efforts of the track crew and the steam crane to right the cars or remove them and get the line cleared for traffic.

The *Carlton County Vidette* reported railroad accidents on an almost weekly basis. One tragic train wreck took place on a Tuesday evening, March 26, 1907, when the northbound Northern Pacific passenger train from Minneapolis to Duluth derailed about a mile and a half southeast of Carlton, due to icy water washing out the earth around a plugged culvert. The engine, tender, and baggage car went off the track, leaving a passenger car partially suspended but still on the embankment. The engineer, Thomas Quinian, and fireman, Arnold Mehsickomer, were killed when the tender landed on the engine cab. The mail clerk was injured, but the passengers were only shaken up. Reverend Guy S. Davis of the Presbyterian Church in Carlton, a passenger on the train, walked to Wrenshall with a lighted flare to warn the westbound freight train coming up from Duluth, thus avoiding a second accident with even graver consequences.

Carlton County Vidette, March 30, 1907.

Derailed diesel near Highway 61 at Carlton, ca. 1951.

Much of the early business of the County Commissioners dealt also with surface roads to Northern Pacific Junction. A road from Thomson to the Junction, including a bridge and sale of $5,000 worth of bonds to pay for it, was approved in March, 1874, as was a road connecting Twin Lakes to Northern Pacific Junction later in June. Moose Lake requested in 1882 that a surface road be built to link its community to Northern Pacific Junction, and the following year a request was made for a road from Knife Falls to Komoko. When these projects were carried out, they effectively duplicated with surface roads what the railroad companies had done with steel tracks—they had placed Northern Pacific Junction at the hub of a great transportation network. In the mid-1880s the only other county road was the early trail that connected the Finnish farming settlements along the Midway River with Thomson. Thus, as the decade of the 1880s unfolded, Northern Pacific Junction became the center of activity in the county. Not surprisingly, public opinion began to support the idea that the county seat should again be moved, this time from the village of Thomson to where the new action was.

Surface roads were improved in the county. This driver is heading south toward Carlton on a well maintained gravel road.
Photo by Nelson Freeman

As early as 1886 there had been a vote to move the county seat to Northern Pacific Junction, but there was no facility in the community that could serve as court house, offices, and jail. Meetings of the Commissioners continued to be held in Thomson, although the County Attorney, Henry C. Oldenburg, protested that the wishes expressed in the vote should be observed. As time passed Cloquet, the booming sawmill town, also emerged as a contender for the role as county seat, it having quickly become the largest settlement in the county. In the summer of 1889 the matter came to a head. On August 26, 1889, Thomas H. Martin submitted a petition signed by over one hundred people requesting that the county seat be moved to Northern Pacific Junction. The following morning at 9:30 a.m. the petition was officially filed at the court house in Thomson. However, later that day a second petition was filed requesting that the county seat be moved to Cloquet. A special meeting of the County Commissioners was called for September 16th to deal with this matter. At this meeting, which went on for three days, William Mayer, board chairman from Northern Pacific Junction, ruled that the petition filed first should be heard first, and he was supported by Thomas McEntee, Commissioner from Mahtowa, and William Oliver, Commissioner from Barnum, but the ruling was opposed by A.W. McDowell, Commissioner from Cloquet, and F.W.

Butters, Commissioner from Thomson. As a result, Northern Pacific Junction was the option placed on a referendum ballot to be voted on October 15, 1889. In that referendum Twin Lakes voted 265 to 0, Mahtowa 39 to 3, and Moose Lake 301 to 0 in support of the move to Northern Pacific Junction, and Thomson voted 1 to 211 and Knife Falls 88 to 337 to oppose. Northern Pacific Junction had won by a vote of 694-551. Harry H. Hawkins, the lawyer representing Thomson, had challenged the validity of the Northern Pacific Junction petition, and following the results of the vote, he then left for St. Paul to obtain a court ruling to have the referendum declared invalid.

At this point the townspeople of Northern Pacific Junction took matters into their own hands. Under cover of darkness, sometime late in 1889, the County Auditor's office was broken into and the safe containing the county records, and numerous other files was taken, placed on a wagon, and carried to Northern Pacific Junction. Because the bridge over the St. Louis River was so shaky the horses were unhitched, led over the bridge, and the wagon was pulled across by ropes. The safe and papers were then hidden in Northern Pacific Junction. Folklore has it that the sheriff also went into hiding so that if ordered by the courts to return the records he would not be found to serve the papers. Were the Paine Lumber Company horses used to pull the wagon? Just who participated in this enterprise is impossible to determine at this date, but it was widely held that many of the community leaders were involved. In the end, the referendum and the petition preceding it were found to be legal and the State Legislature approved the change.

This was not the end of the story, however. There was still no really suitable place for the work of county government to be carried out. Therefore, in 1890 the residents of Northern Pacific Junction voted to approve a $10,000 bond issue to build a new courthouse. This was done and construction was started by the firm of Leck & McLead on the quite beautiful, two and a half story, red brick structure. The courthouse served until 1924.

The Carlton County Court House was built in 1890 of red brick with brown stone trim, in something of the Richardson Romanesque style. This building was replaced by the current court house in 1924.

One final item remained—the name of the town. The village of Northern Pacific Junction had been officially incorporated on November 21, 1881, and Mark Paine, the cousin of Captain Paine, was elected President of the Village Council. The Council consisted of two and later three Trustees, a Recorder, a Treasurer, a Justice of the Peace, and a Constable (other offices were created later). A Village Hall was built the following year. However, as the settlement grew and took on stature, including the new position of county seat, the name Northern Pacific Junction sounded inconsequential. In February of 1891 the *Carlton County Vidette* complained, "N. P. Junction signifies nothing, and Northern Pacific Junction is a name long enough for a garden fence, but implies nothing more than a wayside junction." The paper argued that the community was the business center of growing importance and was "entitled to be recognized as something more than just a railroad crossing." On April 15, 1891, the village council resolved to change the name of Northern Pacific Junction, and in May the Minnesota Legislature authorized the change of the name of the community to Carlton, in recognition of the county and Col. Reuben B. Carlton, after whom it had been named.

The Carlton Village Hall was built of red brick in 1882 at the corner of Chestnut and Third Street. It served as the offices for the town, a center for meetings, the fire hall, and, for a time, even the library. It was taken down in 1936, in part because it obscured vision at the intersection of what had become Highway 61, and was replaced with the Civic Center on Chestnut Street.
Photo couresy of Tim Johnson

The town had changed greatly over the past twenty years. The *St. Paul Daily Pioneer* had reported in November, 1870, that a fire had destroyed three saloons, two liquor stores, one drug store, and one general store. How representative this was is hard to say, but the proportions do conform to the reputation enjoyed by railroad and lumber towns. One young man traveling through Northern Pacific Junction in the spring of 1871, looking for work on the railroad, wrote in his journal that while the scenery was very beautiful, "the junction is a pretty rough place, only about 30 houses all told, looks as if they were all put up in a day. Woods very thick, stumps of trees all around, no streets, not a horse in the place, but lots of men looking for employment." Even in 1887 the *Minneapolis Tribune* noted that there

The red brick Carlton County Jail was built on Walnut Street in 1914. This structure served the county until 1979-80.
Photo by Smith Studio

were ten saloons for a population of five hundred. One of the perennial issues for the town council in the 1880s was the question of liquor licenses—their price, which varied from $50 to $500, and their transfer from one person to another. By 1885 the council insisted on Sunday closing for saloons and no pool playing, singing, dancing, or music on the Sabbath. In 1897 slot machines were banned. Gradually the council also required that horses, mules, cattle, and other domestic animals not be allowed to roam freely in the community, that property owners build wooden sidewalks along their frontage, that

The saloon and hotel run by Michael and Elizabeth Brady in the 1880s. They had both died by the early 1890s, leaving two young daughters to be raised by their aunt, Mrs. John Flynn.

quarantines be established in the event of infectious diseases, and that sanitary conditions be maintained in restaurants and hotels. Fifteen oil burning street lamps were acquired from Marshall-Wells in Duluth in 1893, although the services of a night watchman continued.

By the end of the 1890s Carlton was becoming increasingly established. There were five general stores, four hotels, and only eight saloons. One of the earliest commercial establishments was a general store run by William Dunlap, which preceded the construction of the train depot. An important general store was the J.M. Paine Company store. Operated initially for the lumber company employees, the store carried a substantial variety of goods. James Dunphy also ran "The Big Store," carrying a variety of merchandise, as Maurice Haubner said, "from gifts for brides to heavy farm machinery." The finest hotel in Carlton built in 1880 was a two story wood frame structure, with a long covered porch along the front, called the Riedle House. George Riedle, who also served as postmaster during the Republican administrations of the 1880s, and his wife served meals to twenty-five guests in the hotel's dining room. Asa Paine, the son of Captain J.M. Paine, was president and one of the founders in 1892 of the Carlton County Bank. The bank had paid up capital of $15,000 and performed a variety of financial services,

From 1915 to 1918 Carlton had two banks. The First National Bank was founded in 1903 by the Weyerhaeuser interests from Cloquet and two years later they built the facility to the left, on the corner of Chestnut and Third Street. The Farmers & Merchants Bank was started in 1915, but was sold to the First National Bank in 1918.

including foreign exchange and the sale of stocks, bonds, insurance, and even steamship tickets, but it served largely as a mortgage and loan institution. A new brick building was constructed for the bank, with cherry wood paneling and an enormous Diebold walk-in safe. Captain Paine was also the president of Carlton County Abstract and Title

The Commercial House on east North Street. This was one of the several boarding houses that serviced the salesmen and commercial travelers that regularly visited Carlton as a railroad, lumber, and farming center.

Company. The *Carlton County Vidette* was founded by A. DeLacy Wood in 1887, but it was not until 1891 that a functioning weekly newspaper was published by H.L. Wiard and edited by James S. Mills. The paper had a precarious beginning. It was originally printed in Cloquet and went through several owners, but it became a major institution in both Carlton and the county, surviving up until the 1960s. The *Vidette* served as a strong voice for both Carlton and the rural parts of the county. Advertisements in the *Carlton County Vidette* indicated a variety of services offered in Carlton: Henry Oldenburg, attorney, Alpheus Woodward, attorney, L.A. Sukeforth, physician, Jacob Haubner, blacksmith, Edward Greaves, printer and paper hanger, and many more. By the mid-1890s, nearby Chub Lake emerged as an attractive regional resort. The *Vidette* described the lake as "a beautiful sheet of water around which there has been a large number of fine summer cottages erected." Indeed, the paper reported a steam yacht on the lake and said that Chub Lake drew the "wealthy" from Superior. It also attracted Carlton people such as the Paines and the Oldenburgs, who built cottages, and countless others who went to the lake for swimming, picnics, and dances at the pavilion. Carlton had grown beyond a mere railroad crossing and sawmill town and become a prosperous settled community.

A picnic at Chub Lake in 1908. A team of four horses and a large wagon carried a party of children to Chub Lake for an outing at the popular recreational spot.

Sources:

Carlton County Vidette, October 1, 1892, May 3, 1912, February 21, 1913, June 27, 1913, October 3, 1913, and October 1, 1953.

Haubner, Maurice H. *Pillars of Society.* Privately printed, 1983. P. 13.

Frank Johnson Diary, April 5, 1871, P2217, Minnesota Historical Society Collections.

Minneapolis Tribune, February 18, 1887.

Northern Pacific Papers, Branch Lines, Box 4, File 508, 134.S.10.16.(F), Box 6, File 1510, 134.B.11.2.(F), and Box 36, Vol. 36, 136.E.5.7B; President's file, 137.D.10.7B, file 732-J; Engineering, 134.I.12.7 (B), file 4001; Minnesota Historical Society Collections.

Pomeroy, Richard. "They Swiped the County Seat: Carlton Won Power Struggle," in *Duluth News-Tribune*, August 5, 1973.

St. Paul Daily Pioneer, November 26, 1870.

Thorpe, James. "Carlton Was the Victor," in *Cloquet Pine Knot*, January 28, 1979.

Vos Ellison, Terri. "County Seat Attained 'By Hook or Crook.'" in *Carlton, Minnesota Centennial.* N.p., 1981.

North Street on a winter's day in the early twentieth century. Horses and sleighs still owned the streets. The Walters and Johnson store still fronted on North Street.

An unpaved road was either muddy or dusty. While little could be done about mud, it was possible to sprinkle water on the dirt roads to keep the dust down. In 1910 Forrest Ecklund drove a horse drawn water sprinkler. Photo courtesy of Darold Powers

The United States Postal Service in 1908. William Collver delivered mail in the Carlton area for about ten years. He was paid the rather substantial amount of $80.00 per month, although he had to look after both the delivery wagon and the horses out of that salary as well. Collver also served for a time as the town constable until he left to become a Pinkerton detective on the railroad. From a U.S. Postal magazine, courtesy of Shirley Collver

Standing in the front on the left is Enoch Nicholson, and on the pump handles to the right are Robert Matson, A.M. Brower, J.B. Thomson, and O. Swanson.

The hand pump of the Carlton fire brigade. Until first steam and then gasoline powered pumper trucks were developed and available, hand powered pumps were all that Carlton had for fighting fires.

Robert Matson, in the straw hat, at the reins of a very sporty rig. Matson was a member of the town council, owned pubs in Carlton, Thomson, and Chisholm, and also operated a track for horse racing.
Photo courtesy of Bob Anderson

The Tom Mann Building contained the Duluth Brewing and Malting Company in Carlton. The structure was later expanded to house the Haaken Andreson Blacksmith Shop.

The Carlton County Grain and Produce Company was owned by Mr. Iverson. This building had also functioned as a grain elevator.

The F.A. Watkins farm at Lake Venoah was a large successful enterprise, the product to some degree of his successful ventures in Superior as a lawyer and speculator in the years before the Panic of 1893. The family settled on the farm and survived the hard times of the 1890s, Watkins becoming the highly respected Judge of Probate in Carlton County. Although this photograph shows a special event, the grand scale of the farm is nicely illustrated.

The F.A. Watkins family on the steps of their farmhouse at Lake Venoah in 1893.

Jack Haubner seated on a hay rake, while the horses have their lunch. Although gasoline powered tractors began making inroads at county farms in the 1920s, horses were used to draw farm implements on many farms until the 1940s.
Photo courtesy of Gene Bro

Raising strawberries and other fruit was a successful enterprise in Carlton County in 1895 as it is today. People are shown picking berries on the Bovee farm near Carlton.
The Land of Promise, St. Paul & Duluth Railroad Co. St Paul. 1897, p. 22

Joseph Mayer, a German immigrant, who by 1895 had a prosperous farm outside of Carlton. He was essentially a market gardener, specializing in strawberries which he grew very successfully. The size of his two-story house is a measure of how well he was doing.
The Land of Promise, St. Paul & Duluth Railroad Co. St Paul. 1897, p. 25

The Beattie cottage in 1915. Several additions had been made to the house, and an entry porch was to be constructed later as well. Maytie Beattie is on the far left and Mary Beattie stands on the right.

Gus Moser waits on a well dressed custormer at his meat market. His counter displays a variety of meats and is complete with stools for the comfort of waiting customers.

Gus Moser's Meat Market on Fourth Street and South Avenue. In addition to the store, there was also a barn, chicken coop, and smokehouse. Gus stands in the center, while his assistant is to the right sharpening his butcher's knife.
Photo courtesy of Gene Bro

Gus and Annie Moser, on the left, at their home at the top of the hill on County Road 3, south of Carlton. Their daughter, Anna Mae, sits on the chair with a puppy, in front of Elizabeth and Fred Grunig. The two Grunig boys are seated on the grass. Mrs. Moser and Mrs. Grunig were sisters. Moser was a butcher in Carlton and Grunig a butcher in Cloquet.
Photo courtesy of Gene Bro

Getting ready for the county fair. Fred Clark Smith holds the bridle of his racing horse, "Bird." In a world of horses, everyone was interested in horse racing.
Photo courtesy of Barb Schmidt

The Carlton Cadets, possibly assembled for the funeral of young Carl Oldenburg in 1905.
Photo courtesy of Darold Powers

The county courthouse could be used for social functions. In 1898 it was elaborately decorated, probably for a railroad union banquet.

The Sångkären "Lyran" of the Swedish Evangelical Lutheran Bethesda
Forsarntring, in 1898, wearing traditional dress.

Photo courtesy of Dyhanne Lee

CHAPTER 5

Building a Community

When the twentieth century dawned Carlton was thirty years old and was poised to grow and flourish with the region, but there were also some uphill struggles. The population had reached 612 in 1890, but had slipped back down to 449 by 1900. This was perhaps the result of the Panic of 1893, which produced a sharp economic downturn across the United States, and the effects of that lasted for a long time. The economic engine driving the community, the Northern Pacific Railroad, went into bankruptcy for the second time, although by the end of the decade it had made a significant recovery.

Carlton was an interesting community in terms of its ethnic composition. Many of its leading citizens were Yankees from New England, like Captain Paine and his family, or from the Mid-Atlantic states or the Old Northwest, like Judge Watkins and his family. Others went back to the early settlement in Twin Lakes and along

Carlton in winter, sometime between 1908 and 1915, looking northwest from the rocks. Clearly visible are the school in the upper right and the courthouse in the center. Photo courtesy of Pam Ziebarth

the old Military Road. In its early years the Northern Pacific Railroad had encouraged settlement along its lines from the population in the eastern states. However, both the railroads and the lumber trade drew into Carlton and the surrounding area both Irish and Canadian settlers. The Irish were mixed—both Catholic Irish, that Maurice Haubner remembered with strong Irish brogues, smoking clay pipes and living south of the Paine sawmill—and Protestant Ulster-Scots. As will be shown, a sizable portion of the founders of the Presbyterian Church were from Ulster. Many of the Irish in the lumber trade came to the United States by way of Canada, particularly New Brunswick and Ontario. Both English-Canadians and French-Canadians were to be found in Carlton as well. A slowing economy in Canada in the late nineteenth century led many to seek their fortunes in the United States. French-Canadians had always been a presence in the region, going back to the fur trade. Work in the lumber camps and sawmills attracted many French-Canadians who settled along the south bank of the St. Louis River and in the cutover farmlands south of Carlton. The French-Canadians were prominent in organizing the first Catholic Church in Carlton. Finns, while not numerous in Carlton itself, were early settlers in the county, establishing farmsteads north of Thomson along the Midway River in 1870. Swedes did settle in Carlton, many coming by way of southern Minnesota, following the St. Paul & Duluth Railroad. Native people were present in the Carlton community also. Although the Fond du Lac Reservation was several miles to the west, many Ojibwe people traded at the general store in Komoko, farmed in the area around Hay Lake, Lac la Belle and Lake Venoah, and hunted deer and smoked meat in the region. By the turn of the century Carlton was a diverse community.

Certainly Carlton's fortunes were not helped by a disastrous fire in March of 1900 which destroyed a number of commercial buildings on South Street, the original main street of the settlement, between the railroad tracks and Otter Creek. They were not rebuilt there but on North Street, which was to shift the center of the village life north of the Northern Pacific tracks. The train depot near Third Street was rebuilt further west, extending the town in that direction. Fires were a constant problem for nineteenth century communities, dependent on wood or coal stoves and on oil or gas lamps. Carlton had already had several serious fires in the sawmill and the rail yards.

On January 28, 1914, one of the sources of local pride was destroyed by fire. The Carlton Horse Market, run by Miss Nellie E. Barnard, drew people from all over northern Minnesota and Wisconsin. Miss Barnard ran a farm of 1,000 acres a few minutes'

The Carlton Horse Market in 1899, located on the Webbeking farm south of town. This was a large brick and wood structure. Buyers from all over the region came to Carlton seeking horses.

walk from town, where auctions had been held since 1900 in a large brick horse barn, two hundred feet by fifty feet in size. Well-known auctioneers from as far away as Iowa came to conduct the sales before crowds as large as three hundred people. Bands or orchestras would provide entertainment while potential customers inspected the animals. While a variety of animals would be put up for sale, including racers, trotters, and occasionally cattle, much of the market was made up of teams of heavy draft horses destined for commercial work of one kind or another. Lumber companies, logging operations, and farmers who worked their teams in logging camps were strongly represented at these sales. The fire, which broke out at night, destroyed the barn, a number of horses, several sleighs and buggies, a great deal of tack, and a large amount of feed and supplies. A poultry building was also lost. The value of all of this property amounted to about $17,000. Undeterred by this calamity, Miss Barnard rebuilt her horse barn and was back in operation by the end of March, 1914, drawing in customers from both the local area and as far away as the Iron Range. Miss Barnard also worked in the office of the Register of Deeds and succeeded Captain Paine as the president of the Carlton County Abstract and Title Company.

Schools in Carlton were also plagued by fires. Villagers had petitioned for a school as early as September 18, 1871, so a small wood frame building was constructed on Chestnut Street and Miss Flora Lafan was hired as the teacher. In time, two more teachers were brought in, but in 1895 this school burned and a new two-story, wood frame structure was built. This school had four classrooms and unfortunately, it burned in 1907. A two-story red brick building was constructed in 1908 and five teachers were employed. At the impressive opening ceremonies Senator Moses E. Clapp gave the main address. This school was destroyed by fire on February 16, 1915. The school had been fumigated after an outbreak of scarlet fever and many people assumed that the fire was caused by the fumigation process, but the final conclusion was that faulty electrical wiring started the blaze. The building was a total loss, so a new three-story brick structure was constructed in just under a year's time. Classes were held, meanwhile, in churches, the village hall, the Odd Fellows Club, and the courthouse.

The Carlton School, with students and teachers. The wooden building was built in 1895 in something of the Queen Anne style, with clapboard siding on the first floor and shingles on the second. Spindle work trim decorated the gable ends and a bell tower crowned the building.

By January, 1916, Superintendent C.W. Colovin was able to take possession of a splendid new $42,000 building that featured a gymnasium and auditorium, as well as classrooms, lunch rooms, locker rooms, and offices. A playground and park next door was given by the St. Louis River Water Power Company and named in honor of Jay Cooke. Maurice Haubner remembered Superintendent Colovin fondly, as "a man of principle and integrity," although a strict disciplinarian.

The Carlton School on fire, 1907.

The new brick Carlton School completed in 1908, but itself destroyed by fire on February 16, 1915, as a result of faulty electrical wiring. The church to the right was an early Catholic Church.

The school that didn't burn. This Carlton School was completed in 1916 and has only recently been replaced. The old county jail is seen on the left.

While today children in rural areas, not to mention many urban communities, are bussed to school, that was not possible in the nineteenth century and much of the twentieth. Schools had to be built more or less within walking distance of the prospective students. The first school district in Carlton County was formed at Thomson on October 4, 1870; the school was in a one room wood frame building that also served as a church, Sunday school, and District Court. In 1908 a new school, for three teachers, was built close by. A school was started in Wrenshall in 1894 and a brick building was ready the following year, to which two rooms were added in 1906. This building was replaced by a new school in 1922. Other country schools in the Carlton area were Lone Pine, near Scotts Corner; Hanson, north of Bear Lake; McKinley, in Silver Brook Township; and Barker and Praefke, in Wrenshall Township. Reliable records no longer seem to exist for these schools, although they are named on various maps and are remembered still by those who attended them.

The teacher and children of the Lone Pine School, near Scotts Corner, 1913-1914. From left to right: Adolph Lavigne, Donald Sheff, Russell Walters, David Lavigne, Earl Goman, Howard Goman, Harry Goman, Clare Loban, Vaugh Sheff, Mildred Walters, Ruth Walters, Jean Ferguson, Gladys Loban, Ruth DeRuy, Kathleen Sheff, Merlyn Sheff, Mabel Goman, Helen Sheff, Evelyn Habhegger, Ethel Goman, and the teacher, Helen Lynch.

These fires also prompted the consideration of a proper fire fighting program. As early as 1884 a public meeting was called to organize a "Hook and Ladder Company." At some point a fire pump was acquired, and by 1890 the village records refer to the "Fire Engine House." Indeed, the fire station was also used as a school room and eventually jail cells were attached to it. Nevertheless, the village had a volunteer fire brigade with the capacity to shoot a stream of water on a fire and ladders to scale a burning building. Various types of equipment were acquired from Marshall Wells hardware supply store in Duluth. In 1895, to provide a more extensive supply of water, because municipal water service had not yet been installed, the town negotiated with the St. Paul & Duluth Railroad to have access to their water tower for fire fighting purposes. The railroad company graciously agreed and installed pipes to the tower

Carlton's first motorized fire truck, a 1925 Ford, rebuilt by the men of the Cloquet Fire Department, pictured here at the Cloquet Fire Hall.

that could be connected to hoses. However, even with all of these efforts, the risk of fire remained high, and each major fire prompted new discussions about how to make the Fire Department more effective. Jacob Haubner was appointed Fire Chief in 1894 and he was succeeded by Swan Malmquist.

Concerns for the spiritual needs of Carlton were not far behind the desire for education. Although no church was built until the 1890s, Catholic priests from the Sacred Heart Church in Duluth began coming to Carlton in the 1870s to give services to the Catholic community that was part French and part Irish. In 1886 Father J.B. Genin came to Carlton, but only stayed until 1889. He was followed in 1891 by Father Joseph Mavel, who also served for three years, but who oversaw the building of a small wood

St. Francis of Assisi Catholic Church on Chestnut Street.

frame church on Fourth Street. Three more priests came to serve the Carlton parish, the last of whom, Father John O'Dwyer, attempted to build a larger brick church. This project overreached the capacity of the community, and when the parish was unable to meet the debts owed to the contractors, the unfinished building was sold to the Presbyterians. The old church had to suffice until it burned on August 9, 1928. In part through the generosity of a benefactor from Chicago, a Mrs. Wilhelmine Coolbaugh, construction had already started on Chestnut Street for a new wood frame church to replace it when the fire took place. The new church was called St. Francis of Assisi Catholic Church and the first baptism in it took place in October, 1928.

The First Communion and Confirmation class, together with the priest and bishop, in front of the St. Francis of Assisi Catholic Church in 1941.
Photo by Olson Studio courtesy of Donna Melin

Reverend James A. Paige, the first regular minister at the McNair Presbyterian Church.

The Presbyterians in Carlton felt the need to form a church very quickly after settlement also. They were assisted by Reverend James A. Laurie who in 1873 became the minister of the Rice's Point Presbyterian Church in Duluth. Laurie visited with Presbyterians in Thomson and Northern Pacific Junction both before and after moving to Duluth. He supported the petition to the Synod of Minnesota and the St. Paul Presbytery for the organization of a church at Northern Pacific Junction. This was carried out on November 23, 1879, and the Olivet Presbyterian Church was formed out of a community of nine, five of whom were from Ulster in the north of Ireland.

After Reverend Laurie left for a church in Washington territory, other ministers from Duluth and Cloquet also ministered to the congregation. Reverend R.J. Creswell served Carlton and Cloquet, coming from the mission service in Pembina, North Dakota in 1883. He also served Fond du Lac, Barnum, and Moose Lake, getting from place to place on a railroad velocipede. New members were attracted to the congregation and the need for a church building was strongly felt. A subscription raised $413.82 and the Presbyterian Board of Church Erection donated $500.00, but the gift of a half acre of land on Birch Street and the lumber from W.W. McNair, the local lumberman, and his mother made the building of

The McNair Presbyterian Church in 1885.

James M. Paine Memorial Presbyterian Church, before 1957.

the church possible. On October 19, 1884, the church, re-named the McNair Memorial Presbyterian Church in recognition of the principle contributors, was opened. The church then had a series of successful ministers and growing membership. The Sunday School and youth group were developed, and a Women's Aid Society and Women's Missionary Society were organized. It was under Reverend James Watt that the church was able to acquire the unfinished Catholic church building in 1910 for $2,785.00, thanks largely to the generosity of Mrs. J.M. Paine, the widow of the lumberman. With the willing assent of the McNairs, the name of the church was again changed, now to the J.M. Paine Memorial Presbyterian Church.

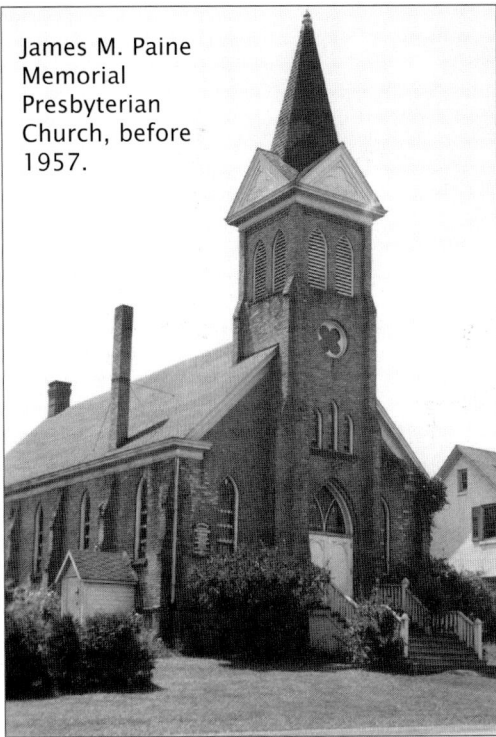

The officers of the James M. Paine Presbyterian Church: M.C. Christenson, J.E. Green, Reverend J.D. Whittles, Robert McFarland, and Neal C. Nickerson.

As the Swedish community began to move into Northern Pacific Junction and Thomson in the 1870s the need arose for Lutheran services. By the early 1880s the Reverend C.J. Collin from Duluth began holding services in Swedish in Northern Pacific Junction and the surrounding region. A meeting to create a congregation was held in the home of A.D. Ecklund in February of 1886 and by November the Swedish Evangelical Lutheran Bethesda Church was organized by the community. The immediate needs were for a pastor and a church building. The Reverend J.B. Bennet was appointed in 1888 and he became the first of several pastors shared with Our Savior's Lutheran Church in Cloquet until 1905. Work also began on building a church. Edward C. Baumann contributed the land on Chestnut Street, for the price of one dollar, and the lumber was purchased from the Andreas M. Miller sawmill in Thomson where many of the church members worked. A structure some 48 feet by 32 feet was completed before the end of the year at a cost of about $3,000. Sunday School was started in 1889 and, along with the choir, became a major program in the church. The Sunday School year reached a grand climax for many with an annual picnic at Chub Lake and boat rides for everyone. The church organized the Ladies Aid, the Women's Missionary Society, the Dorcas Society, the Men's Brotherhood, the Luther League, and a band. A new parsonage was built in 1908 with the assistance of the

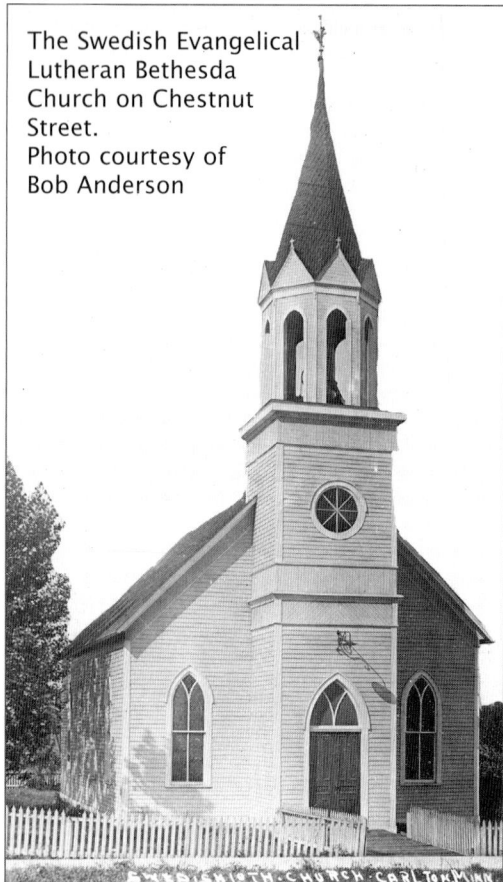

The Swedish Evangelical Lutheran Bethesda Church on Chestnut Street.
Photo courtesy of Bob Anderson

Swedish Lutherans of Mahtowa and Atkinson, who united with those in Carlton in 1909. The Lutherans in Wright also joined the Carlton pastorate in 1912. Services were held in Swedish for years. English was gradually introduced and in 1923 English became the official language of the church. Following some fire damage in 1923 from a kerosene lamp, extensive renovations were undertaken. A basement was constructed and a furnace set

The confirmation class of the Swedish Lutheran Church in 1914. Back, left to right – Esther Anderson, Hulda Lindquist, Tecla Olson, Randie Dahl, Edna Johnson, Lillian Carlson, Mary Trostad, Lillian Wederstrom; front – George Nicholson, Raymond Freeman, Fred Johnson, Pastor E.J. Peterson, Henry Landgren, Julius Magnuson.

The Bethesda Lutheran Bible School class photographed with Reverend Charles Erickson.

in place, electricity was installed, the old clear windows were replaced with stained glass, and the building was given new paint. Four years later modern plumbing, a kitchen, and an assembly room were added at the back of the church building.

A Methodist Episcopal Church was also built along Chestnut Street in Carlton in 1899. However, membership gradually fell off and the church was closed in 1920. The church building was later made into a residence.

The cultural and intellectual life of the Carlton community was not neglected either. The Carlton Women's Study Group was organized in 1915 with the intention "to

Margaret Oldenburg—
teacher, librarian, and
arctic traveler.
Photo by Powers Studio

promote social culture and the betterment of the community." They soon felt that a public library would be a good influence in the town. A managing board was formed with Cordelia Paine as president, Mrs. I.S. Searls as vice president, and Margaret Oldenburg as secretary, and an advisory board was to be appointed later. Books were donated by private individuals (particularly the Oldenburg and Paine families), some were purchased by the Study Group, the town council provided some funds for book purchases, and some were rented from a traveling library. Books were sought in Swedish, Norwegian, German, and other languages, as well as in English. Through the generosity of Miss Paine, the first library was located in the Paine Building on 4th Street. Mrs.

A.M. Brower served without salary as the first librarian and Miss Marie Watkins volunteered to conduct a story hour for children on Saturday mornings. World War I also provided the organizational motivation in order to create a healthy diversion for soldiers stationed in Thomson.

Some time later the library was moved into the town hall at what became Highway 210 and Highway 61, with Mrs. H.V. LeMaster as librarian. In 1924 the Village of Carlton took responsibility for the public library; it was moved to the courthouse and Mrs. LeMaster was given a salary of $20.00 a month. During the Great Depression her salary was reduced to $16.00 a month until 1944 when it was raised again to $20.00. Another attempt to cut costs was made in 1934 when the public library was combined with the school library, but that proved to be illegal and so the organizations were separated in 1937. Also that year the library was moved to the Carlton Civic Center, where it remained until 2005 when it moved to new quarters on Chestnut Avenue. Mrs. LeMaster served as librarian for forty years. The library held over 6,000 books, as well as other media, and in 1967 it joined the Arrowhead Library System which has given Carlton readers easy access to an even larger collection of books. The Study Group remained active into the 1980s.

Career women—Mrs. Julius Baumann, Register of Deeds, and Miss Nora Nilson, County Superintendent of Schools.

The cast of the Carlton School play in 1913, featuring Catherine Gilbert, Ella Nehr, Avis Woodward, Henry Butters, Lottie Dunphy, and Frances Waugh.

The Carlton graduating class of 1930. Back row: Everett Froberg, Gertrude Mann, Helen Summers, Ed Murray, Mary Lavigne, Ruth Lynch, and Lucille Ynedsted. Front row: Dolly Johnson, Helen Christenson, Cliff Haubner, Bernice Smith, and Charlotte Zacher.

Judge F.A. Watkins

Francis A. Watkins was born on April 17, 1853, in Stark, New Hampshire, but as a boy of ten was brought by his family to Baraboo, Wisconsin. He was educated at Lawrence College and the Columbia University Law School in New York, worked in a law office in Hudson, Wisconsin, and was admitted to the bar in Wisconsin and Minnesota. In 1882, at age 29, he moved to Carlton and married Anna Caroline Wieck of Pine City. Watkins began a legal practice in Carlton and in Superior, Wisconsin, where he was very successful in banking and real estate during the boom days prior to the Panic of 1893. In 1890 Watkins bought land from Stephen Dunphy at Lake Venoah and shortly thereafter adjacent pine lands from Captain James M. Paine, and a large farm was built. It was to this farm that he brought his family after a partial collapse of his fortunes in Superior. At the same time his wife's health was failing, despite operations in Chicago and convalescent trips to California. Anna died in 1896, the same year as her father. Watkin's father died the following year. Various neighbors helped with the four children, but Watkins's sister Sara stayed with them and helped until she married the Carlton lawyer J.E. Green. She was followed by Elizabeth Hewlett from Superior. In August 1900, Watkins married Elizabeth and they had one son. During these years Watkins supported himself largely through the farm, but in 1903 he was appointed Judge of Probate in Carlton County, a position to which he was subsequently elected year after year. As Judge Watkins, and as a leader in agricultural development, road improvements, and the welfare of the county, he was regarded as the "Grand Old Man." He died on March 5, 1926. All of the Judge's five children survived him, Walter Olin Watkins, Lucius Harlow Watkins, Wenonah Watkins Tostevin, Marie Siloam Watkins, and Ralph H. Watkins. Lucius Harlow Watkins maintained a lasting connection with Carlton, becoming one of the founders of the Carlton County Historical Society and a leading figure in collecting artifacts and getting them displayed at the Carlton County Fair.

Judge Watkins' brother Dr. Olin S. Watkins was one of the town's early physicians, serving from time to time as health officer. Dr. Watkins also ran for Congress as the candidate of the Public Ownership Party, the socialist party in the state.

At the Election Nov. 4, 1924, Vote for F. A.

WATKINS

FOR JUDGE OF PROBATE

The Probate Court is a Court of Record, the same as the District Court. It is necessary that the Judge have legal knowledge and training.

Issued by F. A. Watkins Carlton, Minnesota.

Campaign poster for F.A. Watkins for election as Judge of Probate. Judge Watkins became something of the "Grand Old Man" of the county and was unbeatable in elections.

Carlton County Vidette

For eighty years the *Vidette* was the voice of Carlton and Carlton County. The exact origins of the paper are lost in time, as there are no surviving records. However, it is understood that in 1887 a frontier entrepreneur, A. DeLacy Wood, started the newspaper in Carlton, as he had in a number of towns. His practice was to get the support of the local merchants, bring in a press and type, get the paper going, and then sell out and move on. This happened with the *Vidette* and after Wood left for Two Harbors, the paper was printed only irregularly until H.L. Wiard took it over. Wiard was a showman, a saloonkeeper, a race horse manager, and a farmer, but on January 17, 1890, he and James S. Mills, as editor, brought out Volume IV, Number 1, of the *Carlton County Vidette*. While this was a modest four page weekly with little local news, it was the practical beginning of the paper. Mills was replaced as editor in 1892 by Thomas G. Graham and the paper itself appears to have gone into receivership to the Asa Paine's Carlton County Bank. D.C. Anderson, a printer from South Dakota, took over and by 1894 appeared on the masthead first as manager and then as editor and proprietor. During Anderson's management the paper remained small, dominated by syndicated news and advertisements, with local comings and goings on the back page. In 1909 Anderson leased the paper to Fred C. Cooper of Moose Lake and in 1910 he formed a partnership with W.H. Hassing, a linotype operator for the *Duluth Herald*. Hassing bought the paper and edited it for four years, but had to leave it because of severe rheumatism. The paper was sold to

In the late 1950s the old *Carlton County Vidette* building was torn down and replaced by larger and more elaborate facilities.

The Carlton graduating class in 1936.
Photo by Olson
Courtesy of Dyhanne Lee

J.V. Barstow in 1914, but Hassing returned and bought back the *Vidette* in 1916 and ran it, with the help of his wife Mavis and his son Bert, until his death in 1945. Hassing made the *Vidette* into a modern newspaper. Local news took the form of articles which appeared on the front page. Syndicated news was cut back and, except for critical events, was placed on page two. News from the various regions in the county appeared in regular columns each week, and Hassing himself wrote a weekly editorial.

Walter H. and James McGenty bought the paper in late 1945 and ran it until Walter died in 1950, when it was taken over by J.R. Van Horn and Bernard H. Ritter, Jr. of the *Duluth Herald and News-Tribune.* These interests in turn sold it in 1953 to Frank Williams, Frank Tibbits, and Alex Bedard, also an out of town group. In 1957 Mansel D. Martin bought out Bedard and eventually acquired the paper and ran it himself for an extended period of time. Throughout these years, the continuity of the paper was held together through the writing and editorial skills of Ruth Finberg.

Ruth Finberg provided continuity at the *Vidette* during the 1950s and 1960s when there was a steady turn-over of owners.

Martin bought new printing equipment and opened an advertising office in Cloquet, eventually publishing the *Cloquet Billboard.* On December 29, 1965, he published the last edition of the *Carlton County Vidette.* Although he kept his printing operation in Carlton, the paper was subsequently released under the title *Cloquet Vidette.* It still printed news from Carlton and the rest of the county, but it was no longer Carlton's newspaper.

Sources

Bethesda Lutheran Church, Carlton Minnesota: 100th Anniversary, 1886-1986. Privately printed, 1986.

Caliguire, Diana, in *Carlton, Minnesota, Centennial.* N.p., 1981.

"Carlton Stock Market Barn Burned Down," *Carlton County Vidette,* January 30, 1914.

Finberg, Ruth, "Down Memory Lane," *Carlton County Vidette,* September 9, 1976.

Haubner, Maurice, *Pillars of Society.* Privately printed, 1983. P. 16.

"History of Carlton Public Library," Carlton County Historical Society.

Holmquist, June Drenning (ed.). *They Chose Minnesota: A Survey of the State's Ethnic Groups.* St. Paul: Minnesota. Historical Society Press, 1981.

J.M. Paine Memorial Presbyterian Church, Carlton, Minnesota, 1879-1979. Privately printed, 1979.

J.M. Paine Memorial Presbyterian Church: Our Church. Privately printed, 1954.

Ledgers of the Secretary of the Carlton Village Council, 1881-1935, Carlton County Historical Society.

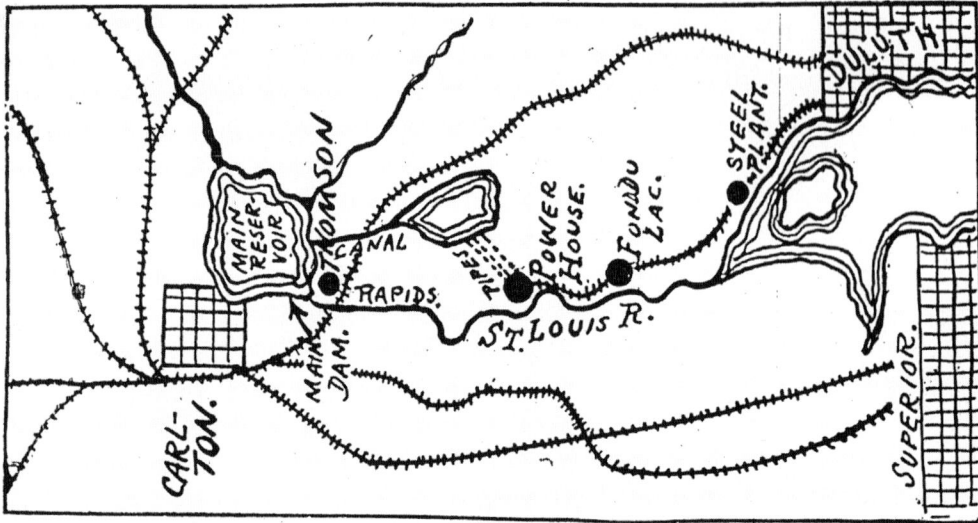
74

CHAPTER 6

Old Legacies and New Directions

The fortunes of the town of Carlton and the region remained linked to Jay Cooke for several generations. Carlton owed its origins to the strategic junction it formed in the railroads that opened up both northern Minnesota and the great transcontinental lines stretching to the Pacific Coast. However, the Panic of 1873 and the financial crisis that followed broke the great banking house of Jay Cooke & Company and also seemed to eliminate the man Jay Cooke from the affairs of Minnesota and the railroads he had dominated—the Northern Pacific, the Lake Superior & Mississippi, and the St. Paul & Pacific. Most of Cooke's assets, including his properties in Minnesota and his homes in Pennsylvania and Ohio, were sold to meet the obligations of the various companies for which he was responsible. In 1873 Cooke was still in his early fifties, however, and a very capable businessman. Discharged from bankruptcy in 1876, he never returned to either banking or management. Living with his daughter and occupying a desk in the office of his son-in-law, Charles D. Barney, Cooke began a steady financial return. Working with no capital of his own, Cooke undertook to negotiate the building of a railroad connecting Salt Lake City with a silver mine in the deserts of Utah. The railroad was built and the mine was a success. For his efforts Cooke was paid in both commissions and stock, earning him altogether about a million dollars by 1880. This was the beginning of a new business career. Jay Cooke was on his way back.

In 1885 Cooke returned to Duluth and began the process of repurchasing some of the properties he had owned before the crash. Among those purchases were parts of the lower St. Louis River valley and parts of the Thomson area. He was back again in September of 1891, ready now to savor the completion of the Northern Pacific Railroad. A private car, the *Minnewaska*, was put at his disposal by the railroad company for his trip across the country. Cooke could claim some considerable credit for the opening up of the north-

Familiar landmarks in early 20th century Carlton—the Thomson dam, the old brick plant, and the automobile and foot bridge over the gorge of the St. Louis River.
Photo by Smith Studio

western part of the United States, from Duluth to the coast. He was fêted wherever he went, particularly in Duluth. The *Vidette* celebrated his presence in Carlton and crowds came out to see him pass through.

One of the first fruits of those acquisitions was the construction of the St. Louis River Slate Brick Company, approximately where the Thomson dam is now located. A small wooden dam was constructed by the company to power a grinder that reduced slate rock to the mud from which bricks could be made. In December of 1891 John M. Butler, Cooke's son-in-law, visited Thomson and the brick plant in order to oversee the manufacture of the first bricks and supervise the payment of wages to the workmen. The company produced a dark red brick that was deemed to be of better quality than pressed brick made from clay, and they could make about 20,000 a day. The second major Cooke enterprise was the formation in the 1880s of the St. Louis River Water Power Company from the lands purchased along the river valley. Throughout these years local people had proposed several projects to either improve the dalles of the St. Louis River for running logs to the sawmills in Duluth and Superior or to dam and divert the waters of the upper St. Louis River to build canals to the crest of the Duluth Hills for power or transportation purposes. Legal, financial, and even diplomatic obstacles rendered these plans unrealizable. However, by the end of the century the development of electrical technology—essentially the transformer—enabled electrical current to be sent by cables over relatively long distances without an unacceptable diminution of power. This made practical the idea of building a hydro-electric power plant in the Thomson area to supply Duluth and the region. Power from the river itself was an idea that Cooke had promoted since the 1870s, and the St. Louis River Water Power Company actually provided power to the St. Louis River Slate Brick Company. However, when that enterprise closed down early in the twentieth century, the St. Louis River Water Power Company sold land to the Great Northern Power Company on which to build the Thomson dam and hydro-electric plant. "When Mr. [J. Horace] Harding [a business partner and member of the family] went to him in 1904 and told him that the plans for harnessing the power of the St. Louis River were complete his eyes filled with tears," Cooke's biographer wrote. "He saw that his dreams were about to be realized." On February 16, 1905, just a few months later, Jay Cooke died knowing, as he said, "The last thing is done."

Work began on the Thomson facility in 1905 and it was one of the most sophisticated engineering projects of its day. A three hundred sixty-eight foot dam, thirty-eight feet high and six feet deep, and a one thousand foot concrete spillway were built on a ridge of slate rock that originally formed a waterfall in the river at Thomson. This dam created a service reservoir of about 130 million cubic feet of water, transformed Carlton Lake into Thomson reservoir, pushed the mouth of the Midway River well to the north, and raised the water level significantly above the town of Thomson. The objective of all this was to channel water through a relatively level canal to a point where, through a

FALLS OF THE GREAT NORTHERN WATER POWER PLANT AT THOMSON, MINN.

precipitous drop, the water rejoined the river several miles down stream, passing through powerhouse turbines on the way. The canal, fifteen feet deep and seventy feet wide, was dug from a point between Thomson and the new mouth of the Midway River east for about a mile and a half along the Northern Pacific "Short Line" track to a Forbay lake. A dam and headgate at the end of the Forbay directed the water into three penstocks made of redwood staves seven feet in diameter and five thousand feet long—like three long wooden barrels—and downhill roughly three hundred and fifty feet to the powerhouse at the river's edge. The water, under great pressure, thanks to its descent, then passed through turbines that turned two generators producing 30,000 horsepower of electricity. The Thomson powerhouse held what were then the largest 60,000 volt, three phase transformers ever built. "PRODIGIOUS WATER POWER OF ST. LOUIS RIVER SECOND ONLY TO THAT OF NIAGARA," was the claim of the *Vidette*. Transmission lines were built into substations in Duluth, with power coming fully on line in 1908.

The penstocks were placed in trenches, extending from the head gates at the end of the canal, and then buried. They can be seen from the highway when driving past the Forbay facility. The buildings of Forbay are pictured on the left.

The metal portion of the penstocks can be clearly seen in the trenches prior to burying. The penstocks were 5,000 feet long from the head gates to the power station. The stand pipe towers for overflow water are in the center.

A huge penstock, seven feet in diameter and constructed of redwood, channeled water into each waterwheel in the power station. When replaced in 1970, after being buried for over sixty years and under extreme water pressure, the redwood was still in excellent condition.
Photo by Hugh McKenzie courtesy of Minnesota Power

Part of the Thomson hydroelectric power station under construction in 1906.
Photo courtesy of Minnesota Power and MN DNR

Water from the Thomson reservoir was diverted along a 1.6 mile canal to a set of head gates, shown under construction here. The water was then channeled down the three iron and wooden penstocks, seen on the right, 378 feet to the turbines in the hydroelectric station at the rivers edge, producing 13,500 horsepower. This was one of the largest and most advanced engineering projects of its day.   Photo courtesy of Minnesota Power and MN DNR

The Thomson hydroelectric station at the side of the St. Louis River. The penstocks can be seen covered with earth on the hill and the stand pipe towers are behind them.

The control panel at the Thomson hydroelectric station.
Photo courtesy of Tim Johnson

The Thomson power station and the Forbay community along the St. Louis River.

To carry out all construction work, train tracks were built to the site of the powerhouse. A great deal of bedrock had to be blasted to clear the ground for both the canal and the powerhouse. Almost all of the generating equipment had to be specially built, and some of it failed during installation and had to be replaced. As a result the work was almost a year behind schedule, but it was successfully completed. Because the Thomson powerhouse was so remote at the time, the company built houses for the workmen and

The Forbay School was constructed for the children of employees at the power station. The school was built in 1917 before there were any effective roads into the little community and operated until 1931.

A pleasant August picnic at the Forbay community in 1914. The large white building was a hotel for unmarried men working for the company.

managers and their families, creating what became known as the Forbay community. A school was maintained for the children until 1931, after which they were sent to the Lincoln School in Esko. There were no surface roads into the area at the time either, so the company maintained a kind of trolley—a self-powered Mack Gas Rail Car—for the community and Fond du Lac.

A track had been built from Duluth to the Thomson hydroelectric station during the construction of the facility. Minnesota Power and Light subsequently used a Mack Gas Rail Car for transportation in and out of the Forbay community until practical surfaced roads were built in the late 1920s.

In 1923-24 a second dam and hydro-electric plant was built, several miles down river from the Thomson powerhouse. This Fond du Lac dam formed a gentle curve from one side of the St. Louis River to the other, five hundred feet long and eighty feet high—the south side in Carlton County and the north side in St. Louis County, thanks to a jog in the boundary. As with the Thomson system, the powerhouse was located at some distance below and to the side of the dam and was connected by a cast iron penstock eighteen feet in diameter and two hundred ninety-five feet long, creating a head of between 71.5 and 81.5 feet, depending on the variable level of the river. The powerhouse had three-phase, 60,000-volt General Electric generators capable of producing 15,000 kilowatts. Transmission lines were again extended into Duluth and by the summer of 1924 were fully operational. On October 26, 1923, the

Construction of the Fond du Lac dam in 1923-24. This dam was 500 feet long and 80 feet high. As a result of a variation in the boundaries, on one side of the river the dam was in Carlton County and the other side St. Louis County.
Photo courtesy of Tim Johnson

Duluth Edison Electric Company was reorganized as the Minnesota Power & Light Company. The large regional electric company was created out of six smaller utility companies, including the Great Northern Power Company.

When Jay Cooke's firm, the St. Louis River Water Power Company, sold the land for the Thomson dam and hydro-electric station to the Great Northern Power Company in 1904, a few months before Cooke died, it retained much of the river valley between Thomson and Fond du Lac. This included the spectacular gorge through which the river flowed in a riotous torrent of white water, the dramatic outcrops of the Thomson formation which were a prize geological site, and an extensively forested area that was a habitat for a variety of animals, including deer and bald eagles. Historically this was a particularly rich area for the region. Through the St. Louis River valley passed the ancient trails of the Sioux and the Ojibwe, and it also held the Grand Portage of the French explorers of the seventeenth century and the voyageurs of the eighteenth and nineteenth centuries, as they made their way west to the Mississippi River and north to the Rainy River. It was up this river valley that the track for the Lake Superior & Mississippi Railroad had reached in 1870, but these tracks had not been used since 1894 when one of the trestles had burned.

Interest in making something of the river valley began to take shape by the autumn of 1912. On September 8th a party of community leaders from Carlton, Cloquet, and Duluth met in Thomson and walked the five miles along the right of way beside the river to Fond du Lac. The group included Judge F.A. Watkins, Henry C. Oldenburg, W.M. Cain, J.E. Green, from Carlton; Judge William A. Cant, George W. Cooley, engineer for the State Highway Commission, and H.V. Eva, secretary of the Commercial Club, from Duluth; and R.M. Weyerhaeuser, C.I. McNair, Jr., J.E. Diesen, County Attorney, and F.D. Vibert, editor of the *Pine Knot*, from Cloquet. In Fond du Lac they enjoyed a long lunch and concluded that a road should be built along the old Lake Superior & Mississippi railroad bed. Engineer Cooley said that the idea was excellent and that as soon as possible the plan should be presented to the Highway Commission, the Great Northern Power Company, and the Northern Pacific Railroad. The *Duluth News-Tribune* published articles in favor of a road through the river valley in early 1913, but the Northern Pacific was not willing to commit itself about the old road-bed. Not until early 1915 did a public discussion of the idea resume, when the *Vidette* and the *News-Tribune* ran long articles extolling the unique geological and historical features of the St. Louis valley. Jay Cooke's heirs, through the St. Louis River Water Power Company, offered 2,350 acres of land to the State of Minnesota to be made into a park subject to several conditions, including the continued operation of the hydro-electric plants and the right to run power lines through the park. The offer was complicated by the need to pay some $18,017 in back taxes, which the *Vidette* thought was

Carlton saw itself as the gateway to Jay Cooke State Park. This elaborate entrance structure made the statement.

beneath the dignity of Jay Cooke himself. However, local support for a park was so strong that businessmen from Carlton, Cloquet, and Duluth raised a subscription to solve that problem. The Minnesota legislature passed an appropriations act in 1915 creating Jay Cooke State Park and authorizing $15,000 to be used to purchase an additional 4,000 acres of adjacent land, although only 925 acres was acquired at the time. An advisory park commission was created, chaired at the request of the governor by Henry C. Oldenburg, the Carlton lawyer who had handled much of the negotiations with the Cooke heirs. On October 23, 1915, Oldenburg deposited the deed to the land from the St. Louis River Water Power Company with J.B. Baumann, the Registrar of Deeds in Carlton. Just over a year later, on November 1, 1916, F. Rodney Paine, a Yale Forestry School graduate, was appointed park superintendent and secretary to the commission. Jay Cooke State Park came into being.

When Jay Cooke Park was created in 1915 the river valley was surprisingly remote. The old Lake Superior & Mississippi Railroad tracks had been taken up, although there were tracks into the Thomson power station from Fond du Lac. The Northern Pacific Short Line tracks to West Duluth Junction skirted the park to the north, and the Northern Pacific and Great Northern tracks into Superior skirted the park to the south. However, there were no surface roads into the park and therefore not much accessibility. As the historian Roy W. Meyer points out, the immediate problem for Superintendent Paine was to build roads. Partly as a result of the priorities of World War I, by 1920 the road had only extended about two and half miles down the old railroad right of way out of Thomson (and this had cost $9,000). The legislature allocated $10,000 per year for road building in 1923 and 1924 and much work was done. The City of Duluth, which had acquired a substantial amount of property on the eastern border of Jay Cooke Park and created Fond du Lac Park, began building a road from the east. Building surface roads through the St. Louis River valley in the 1920s proved as difficult and expensive as building rail lines through the area in the 1870s, but by 1925 there was only a mile and a half separating the two roads. Eventually the state took over responsibility for the road and it became the eastern end of State Highway 210. By the late 1920s Becks Road and Duluth Skyline Parkway were also linked to the park.

The first swinging bridge at Jay Cooke State Park.

The second need for the park was that of facilities. Superintendent Paine began creating hiking trails as soon as he took office and by 1928 there were some ten miles of trails though the park. The Forest Service built the first of a series of suspension bridges, "swinging bridges," over the river in the mid-1920s. Before that the only way across the river was a footbridge suspended over the river at the Thomson power station, restricted to park workers. The new bridge gave visitors to the park wonderful views of the rapids of the river and the

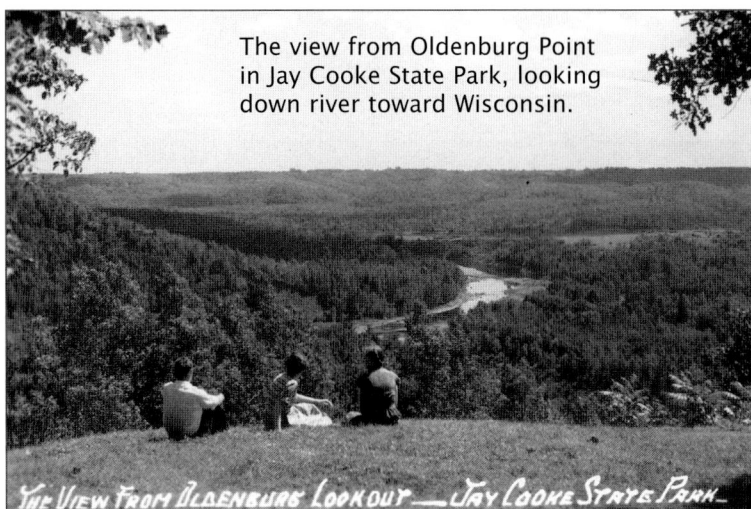

The view from Oldenburg Point in Jay Cooke State Park, looking down river toward Wisconsin.

rock formations and allowed for hiking on the south side of the river, but it was vulnerable to the spring floods and washed out periodically. In 1929 Oldenburg Point was named after the Carlton lawyer who had facilitated the creation of the park. Paine served as superintendent until 1931, which was really the beginning of a new era. The widespread distress caused by the "Great Depression" led to the creation of the Civilian Conservation Corps under the administration of President Franklin D. Roosevelt. The CCC attempted to get young men off the streets, give them proper food and shelter, teach some employment skills, and pay a modest wage. A CCC camp was built in Jay Cooke Park near Forbay Lake. The young men of the CCC built numerous trails, roads, bridges, and picnic sites. Most notably they rebuilt the Swinging Bridge and built the outstanding stone and log structures at Oldenburg Point and the River Inn at the park headquarters. All of these facilities made Jay Cooke Park a favorite destination for picnics, hikes, and sight-seeing. In August of 1935 a pageant was organized in Jay Cooke Park and Fond du Lac to celebrate the importance of the fur trade to the history of the region. A reconstruction of the American Fur Company post was built at Fond du Lac and some 15,000 people came to hear Governor Floyd B. Olson and

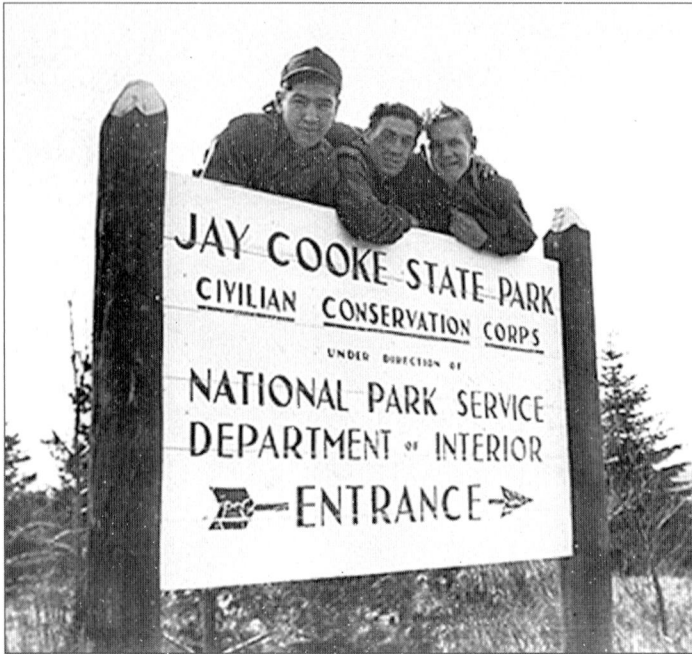

The entrance to the CCC Camp at Jay Cooke State Park.
Photo courtesy of MN DNR

Raymond Moley, one of Roosevelt's "Brains Trust," representing Vincent Astor and the Astor family. Plans were also put in motion to bring more adjacent land within the park, and this was done by both tax-forfeiture, largely from the railroads and the power company, and through purchase. Currently the size of the park is about 8,813 acres, making it the fourth largest park in the state. Jay Cooke State Park placed at Carlton's fingertips one of the showplaces of the state.

Work on the swinging bridge at Jay Cooke by the CCC boys in the 1930s. The bridge, in addition to being an attraction in itself, opened the south bank of the river to wonderful new hiking trails. Photo courtesy of MN DNR

Through Jay Cooke State Park, the Thomson dam and the hydro-electric plants along the St. Louis River, as well as the railroad lines through Carlton, the legacy of Jay Cooke reaches from the 1870s right into the present. Jay Cooke, in the course of a long career in banking, investment, and business, made a lasting impression on both this community and the nation.

The refectory (now known as the River Inn Visitors Center), the swinging bridge, and the Dalles of the St. Louis River, as seen from above.   Photo courtesy of Delphi Oswell

Jay Cooke State Park

"The trip west from Fond du Lac began with a nine-mile carry which became known by the same name as the big carry at the Pigeon, the Grand Portage. The same trail or something like it can be followed by automobile today on a drive through Jay Cooke State Park between Fond du Lac and Carlton. The road winds now near the river and then back in the hills, coming out occasionally on a point high above the rocky river-rushing gorge itself, sometimes going along the side of a hill following the stream but well above it and away from the masses of rocks that edge it. And at the end of the Grand Portage the canoe travelers were able to load for six miles of smooth river travel before they had to unload again to make a new portage, Knife Portage, which was given its name because the rocks along the way stood on edge and cut moccasins and feet. ... All along the rapids in Jay Cooke Park this kind of stone formation can be seen. Right under the walking-bridge across the river at the picnic site by the refectory you can see the river running the length of these great stones which heave out of the ground in rows and layers like oversize shale, sharp and rugged. There was a very lot of rough country to walk through along the St. Louis River portages."

Erling Larsen, *Minnesota Trails: A Sentimental History* (Minneapolis: T.S. Denison & Company, 1958), p. 43.

Henry C. Oldenburg

Henry C. Oldenburg was born in Green Bay, Wisconsin, on September 18, 1858. He was educated at Ripon College, studied law at the University of Wisconsin, and worked in the law office of Robert M. Lafollette. Oldenburg married Mary E. Lamson of Seymour, Wisconsin, in 1888, and they had two children, Carl who died at age eight and Margaret. The family moved to Carlton where Henry established a successful law practice, representing, among others, J.M. Paine in Carlton and the Northern Lumber Company of Cloquet and other Weyerhaeuser interests. Oldenburg also took a keen interest in public affairs, serving as President of the Carlton Village Council in 1891 and 1892 and, being particularly drawn to conservation, as a member of the Minnesota State Forestry Board. He was a key figure in the negotiations leading to the creation of Jay Cooke State Park and once it was operational he chaired the park commission. In 1929, one of the outstanding promontories overlooking the St. Louis River was named Oldenburg Point in recognition of his contributions. The family built a large house in Carlton, which is still standing, and a summer cottage at Chub Lake. The house was in the Italianate style with a veranda on three sides and was made of Wrenshall brick with a roof of slates from Thomson. The grounds were beautifully landscaped with the serene centerpiece of the morning glory pool. Oldenburg died on April 17, 1926, in Charleston, South Carolina, and had a large funeral in Carlton. Both the J.M. Paine Memorial Presbyterian Church and the Bethesda Lutheran Church were used for the services and many leading figures from Carlton, Cloquet, and Thomson participated.

Henry C. Oldenburg—lawyer and civic leader.
Photo by Carl Thiel

The Oldenburg house, showing the celebrated "Morning Glory Pool," one of the showplaces of Carlton.
Photo by Smith Studio

Oldenburg's only daughter Margaret graduated from Vassar College and the University of Minnesota. Although she originally left Carlton to be a teacher, she became a librarian at the University of Minnesota, both at the Geology Department and the main library. Margaret Oldenburg, having been introduced to the wilderness and camping by her father while a girl, sought out adventure through travel. In 1939 she sailed from Montreal on the Hudson Bay Company ship *R.M.S. Nascopie* to the Arctic and back to Halifax, recounting her adventures in September to the Carlton Study Club. Margaret was particularly drawn to the Canadian Arctic, which she visited year after year. Once while staying in Aklavik, near the Mackenzie River in the Northwest Territories, Oldenburg served for several weeks as a nurse to the Native community's only doctor during a flu epidemic. On another occasion, after doing geological research at Yellowknife, a thousand miles north of Edmonton, Alberta, her airplane went down and she was given up for lost, only to be found by a Canadian Pacific Airlines plane. Margaret Oldenburg died in St. Paul in August 1972 and was buried in Carlton.

Margaret Oldenburg in cap and gown in 1921 when she graduated from Vassar College.
Photo by Rydholm Studio

Sources:

Beck, Bill. *Northern Lights: An Illustrated History of Minnesota Power.* Duluth: Minnesota Power, 1985. Pp. 81-102 and 197.

Carlton County Vidette, 1900-1916.

Fritzen, John. *The History of Fond du Lac and Jay Cooke Park.* Duluth: St. Louis County Historical Society, 1978.

Larson, Henrietta M. *Jay Cooke: Private Banker.* Cambridge: Harvard University Press, 1936.

Meyer, Roy W. *Everyone's Country Estate: A History of Minnesota's State Parks.* St. Paul: Minnesota Historical Society Press, 1991. Pp. 45-49.

Northern Pacific Railroad Papers, President's File, J.I. Thomas to R.W. Clark, Janurary 30, 1913, and Clark to Thomas, February 4, 1913, 137.F.5.9 (B), file 1989, Minnesota Historical Society.

Oberholtzer, Ellis Paxton. *Jay Cooke: Financer of the Civil War.* New York: Augustus M. Kelley, 1968 [first published 1907]. Pp. 511-48, quotation from p. 545.

A street scene in Carlton in the 1920s.

With the advent of the automobile, businesses such as Carlton Motors, pictured here in 1928, became important in the community. From left to right: Joe Storey (?), Clara Holm (owner), Walter Dunphy, Arnold Larson, Henry Webbeking, Bill Gillespie, Bill Olson, Carl Hanson, Jim (or Joe) Zacher, Reynold Johnson.   Photo by Kuhn

CHAPTER 7

Carlton's Coming of Age

The first half of the twentieth century saw Carlton come of age. Although the population had fallen in 1900 to four hundred forty-nine, it was up again in 1910 to five hundred ninety-seven and in 1920 to seven hundred. All of this growth meant that the frontier atmosphere that had characterized the early railroad settlement and lumber town had to give way to a more settled and, dare we say it, respectable community. Carlton needed those institutions and services that would produce a rewarding quality of life—what today would be called "community infrastructure." The organization of a village council in 1881, a fire department in 1884, and a public school as early as 1871, arguably the basic necessities for even a frontier settlement, have already been mentioned. Other improvements and refinements were needed.

Public health was a serious consideration in the late nineteenth century. One of the first acts of the village council in 1881 was to pass an ordinance to limit the spread of small pox, diphtheria, and other infectious diseases by requiring that infected people be quarantined for a period of time to allow the illness to run its course. In 1884 Dr. Olin S. Watkins was appointed the first head of the Board of Health with powers to look after the welfare of the town's people. From time to time the health officer asked the village council to take action regarding various restaurants, boarding houses, and hotels because of unsanitary conditions that threatened the health of their patrons and the community. The Board of Health was also anxious about the problem of what to do about garbage. A garbage dump was created and people were expected to burn their garbage there, rather than in their back gardens. A scarlet fever epidemic in 1896 led to the construction of a "Pest House" where infected people could be lodged until sufficiently cured to be allowed back into the community. Carlton was unusual in enjoying the services of a woman doctor for several years. Dr. Inez Legg, a graduate of the Women's Medical College of the New York Infirmary, practiced medicine in Carlton between 1895 and 1904. She came to Carlton from Hinckley where she survived the great fire in 1894.

Dr. Olin Watkins was the younger brother of Judge Watkins. He served as the local physician and from time to time as the town health officer. He also ran unsuccessfully for Congress as a socialist candidate.

Somewhat related to matters of public health was the control of the liquor trade and the operation of public houses. Another of the first acts of the village council in 1881 was to require licenses for the sale of liquor and the operation of billiard tables. With a large population of young, single men, connected with the railroads and the lumber industry, the matter of controlling the operation of public houses presented an ongoing problem. Northern Pacific Junction, and subsequently Carlton, developed something of a reputation for being a wide open town. On August 28, 1878, the *Stillwater Gazette* quoted the *Duluth Herald* reporting that on the previous Sunday in Northern Pacific Junction, "Nearly everybody was drunk, and free fights were the order of the day." The paper concluded, "It looked like old times." The village council, while continuing to issue liquor licenses, struggled to deal with this kind of situation. In 1885 liquor licenses were raised to $100.00 and saloon keepers were warned to keep their doors closed on Sundays and not to permit any pool playing, music, or dancing on their premises. In 1887 the license fee was raised to $500.00 for the ten saloons in town. Several decades later, in 1913, the village council passed a similar ordinance closing saloons on Sundays and election days, as well as between 11:00 p.m. and 5:00 a.m. on weekdays, and ordering that they leave their window curtains open so it could be seen that they were not serving customers. In 1897 the Workhuser Building was simply boarded up and saloon keepers with slot machines were told to get them out of town within twenty-four hours or lose their licenses. Women were forbidden from frequenting saloons in 1907, and in a somewhat related ordinance in 1914, the Tango and other "objectionable dances" were forbidden within the town limits. Local tradition would indicate that there were also many prostitutes working out of some of the saloons and boarding houses, although the village council records are silent on that matter. The question of issuing liquor licenses and allowing the transfer of licenses from one person to another occupied the council year after year. In 1914 the license fee was raised to $1,000.00 per year.

The ladies of the Women's Christian Temperance Union—Mrs. Moore, Mrs. Shogren, Annie Nyquist, Mrs. Habhegger, and Mrs. Andrew Widell. The WCTU was an organization of considerable force in the early years of the century. It led the efforts to tame the frontier character of much of the mid-west and west. Its influence can be seen in the vote in Carlton County to go "dry" several years before "Prohibition" was adopted nationally. Photo courtesy of Vicki Kerttula

Carlton was clearly split on the question of drink. The Women's Christian Temperance Union was active in the town and published a regular column in the paper. Furthermore, these ladies were not without influence. They were joined by the Business Men's Protective Association, which argued that taxpayers had to bear the burden of all the liquor related court costs and jail expenses. Opposition to saloons had driven up the license fee and threatened to prohibit the sale of alcoholic beverages altogether. The March, 1914 municipal elections returned a "wet" village council by a narrow margin. The *Vidette* hoped that the election which had been won "fair and square" would end the bickering and allow things to return to normal. The issue did not die, however. Just over a year later, in May of 1915, the county as a whole voted to prohibit the sale of alcohol, 1,953 to 1,123. Only Cloquet and Scanlon voted wet. Carlton went 95 to 53 in favor of prohibition. It was to go into effect when current liquor licenses expired or at the end of six months time—November 23rd, 1916. This was really the end of Carlton as a frontier town.

More prosaic matters had to be dealt with also. As early as 1884 it was recognized that the town needed sidewalks. Three years later an ordinance was passed requiring all property owners to build a wooden sidewalk in front of their property. All eligible voters were required to pay $1.50 to contribute to the upkeep of the sidewalks or to give one day's labor. By 1892 the sidewalks were generally completed. However, wooden sidewalks deteriorate rather quickly, so in 1908 the village council discussed the possibility of constructing concrete sidewalks. By the 1920s, as the streets were being paved, concrete sidewalks were put in as well.

Putting in water and sewer pipes in 1915 along Chestnut Street was a major undertaking, but it had to be done.

Free ranging animals constituted another problem that marked the transition from a rural settlement to an urban community. In 1897 cattle wandering in the streets, even if wearing bells, were declared a nuisance. In 1903 a shed was built to impound stray cattle, where they would be held until their owners paid a fine. The same year free ranging pigs were also considered a nuisance and a health hazard. The following year, stray dogs, always a problem, were simply ordered to be shot. And as late as 1911 an ordinance was passed making it illegal for chickens to run free on the streets. The owners of stray chickens were liable for fines of no less than $1.00 nor more than $25.00 or possible imprisonment. Another problem for which time has provided no solution was that of reckless speeding through the town. In 1908 speed limits were placed on both horses and automobiles in Carlton, and in 1912 a limit of 8 miles per hour was placed on all vehicles, horse drawn or gas powered. An attempt to place similar speed restrictions on trains passing through the town probably met with less success. The village council also requested the railroads to cease sounding steam whistles and blowing off steam valves within the town limits.

In 1893 Carlton put in fifteen new oil burning street lights to provide some illumination at night. Technology, however, was changing rapidly at the end of the nineteenth century and discussions were held about the possibility of introducing electricity. A committee composed of Henry Oldenburg, John Newquist, and Thomas McCausland was struck by the village council to study the question of how best to acquire electrical power for the town. The Sauntry-Cain sawmill had electric lights, powered by generators run by their steam plants and Martin Cain offered to provide electricity to the town for one year at cost if the village council were willing to accept a longer term arrangement. No action seems to have been taken on that offer and in 1901 the Cloquet Electric Company, a subsidiary of the Cloquet Lumber Company, ran wires into Carlton and provided commercial electrical service. By 1906 the old oil street lamps were replaced with electric street lights. The Cloquet Electric Company, renamed the General Light and Power Company, eventually merged with the Minnesota Power Company of Duluth, and provided electrical power for the whole town of Carlton.

Telegraph service had been introduced with the building of the railroads, but the development and widespread use of the telephone came several decades later. The American Telegraph and Telephone Company, AT & T, had requested permission to run wires through Carlton in 1896. In 1900 the Sauntry-Cain Company, which had a telephone connection with its facilities in Barnum, offered telephone service to the town.

"Number please? Thank you, operator. Give me number 29." The first telephones required a central operator to connect you with the party being called. Before the Northwestern Bell Telephone system was consolidated, Carlton had two telephone companies. This is the telephone exchange building around 1930.   Photo - MHS

Indeed, it appears that some people in Carlton were hooked up to the Sauntry-Cain system. However, in 1901 a two year franchise was given to Charles F. Leland to install a telephone line in Carlton. This service seems to have been extended for some time. In 1910 the Duluth Telephone Company brought long distance lines into the town. Carlton had two telephone systems from 1905 to 1919, the Zenith Telephone Company and the Bell Telephone Company, and a phone from each company was needed to be able to call everyone in the town. The two were consolidated through the Northwestern Bell Telephone system in 1919.

A major capital investment for any community is the construction of water and sewer facilities. As in almost all rural communities water was obtained from wells. For the fire protection of the town, this proved to be most inadequate, and in 1895 Carlton negotiated with the St. Paul & Duluth Railroad to use its water tower in the event of a fire in the town. (The railroad relied on both its own well and the Otter Creek to keep the water tower full.) Private citizens, however, simply dug wells in their back yards. As for sewer facilities, the outdoor privy was the universal solution. One obvious potential problem was the proximity of the wells to the privies. Over time the water wells stood in danger of being contaminated by the nearby privies. There was an aesthetic problem also. The privies smelled, particularly during a long hot summer. Maurice Haubner, recalling the Carlton of his childhood, remembered the outhouses that had "smells that would make your eyes water." In 1908 the village council began to consider building water and sewer facilities for the town, but it was not until 1918 that a water and sewer ordinance was passed. The town had to borrow money through the sale of bonds to pay for the work, but by 1921 construction was started to build the facilities, including putting in underground pipes to private houses and the construction of the landmark water tower.

Commerce drove these civic improvements, and there was a thriving business community in Carlton. A second bank was founded in 1903. On September 29 the First National Bank of Carlton was incorporated with $25,000 in paid up capital. Two Cloquet lumbermen were the chief officers, Rudolph M. Weyerhaeuser was president and C.L. Dixon was vice president, but John F. Hynes of Carlton was the cashier. In 1905 a brick building was erected for the bank at the corner of Chestnut Street and Third Street. Just ten years later the Farmers & Merchants Bank of Carlton was started. It was also linked to Cloquet through the interests of the Northwestern State Bank there. James A. Gillespie was the cashier. However, in April of 1918 the Farmers & Merchants Bank sold its assets to the First National Bank of Carlton. Gillespie became the cashier at the First National Bank and Guy C. Smith, who had succeeded Hynes as cashier, transferred to the First National Bank of Cloquet as cashier. Hynes returned as president in 1919. Carlton people gradually filled the positions on the board of directors: Henry C. Oldenburg, O.F. Walters, J.E. Green, A.H. Lee, and A.B. Loban. While these banks provided a variety of services, including savings deposits, they focused largely on farm mortgages and short-term business loans.

Ray A. Butts, the president of the First National Bank, at the door of his large walk-in safe, in May 1941.

The Carlton Grain and Produce Company was originally part of the J.M. Paine company store and dated from the 1870s. Its primary product was feed for farm animals, but the operation also bought produce from farmers, sold it on a larger market, and

The Carlton Feed Mill was originally part of the J.M. Paine enterprises. Although it has changed hands several times and evolved to meet modern needs, the feed mill still survives.

shipped it out. This helped to make Carlton a farm service center. In 1908 the facility was leased from the Paine estate by James A. McFarland, Nellie Barnard, and Donald McDonald, although McFarland eventually took it over and renamed it the Carlton Mill and Elevator. This firm remained in the McFarland family until 1953 when it was sold to Robert E. Roley who created the Roley Feed and Supply Company.

James Dunphy's "Big Store" on South Street continued to be a major department store in Carlton until it was completely destroyed by fire in January, 1917. In addition to selling such consumer goods as clothing and hardware, the store also sold large items such as farm implements and automobiles. Some of this business was taken over by sev-

The Hultman & Carlson general store in the early twentieth century. Heavy planks made up the wooden sidewalk. These sidewalks made a lot of noise, but they kept people out of the mud.

No shopping cart and self check out here. In the Hultman & Carlson store you could get almost anything you wanted, but you had to tell the clerk and he would get it from the shelf or the counter.

eral other establishments in Carlton. Hultman & Carlson sold general merchandise, high quality dry goods, shoes, groceries, hardware, and crockery. Ecklund & Ivarson, later H. Ivarson Merchandise, ran a substantial clothing store. In 1908 he opened a glove factory in Carlton and sold the clothing store to O.F. Walters of Carlton and G. Johnson of Woodville, Wisconsin. Walters & Johnson became a successful Carlton store. In February of 1910 Ivarson moved his glove making factory to Duluth. S.S. Johnson ran a store that mixed groceries, produce, and fruit with watches, clocks, jewelry, and silverware. In 1908 Johnson specialized in the jewelry business and sold the grocery and fruit business to Harry Sheils and James Gillespie. These two entrepreneurs were bought out the following year by James Dunphy. A cigar factory was started in 1913 by Carl Foasberg, manufacturing and selling the "Lady Como" for 10 cents and the "Carlton" for 5 cents. During these years Carlton also had two livery stables, several meat markets, a lumber yard, a tailor, a shoemaker, several builders and contractors, and a variety of other small businesses.

"Shoemaker, stick with your last." Mr. Karnowski is shown at his last in his Carlton shop in 1929. Calendars and pictures of fashionable ladies adorn the walls and a pot-bellied stove keeps him warm. Thick hides of leather are on the counter. Oh, and the shoes will be ready on Wednesday.

The S.S. Johnson jewelry store was one of the well-known and long-lasting businesses in Carlton. Johnson himself stands on the left, next to a prominent display of pocket watches in the window of his store.

The social and cultural life of the community was not forgotten either. Social groups flourished, such as the Odd Fellows, the Priscillas, the Carlton Fraternity Club (with their popular St. Patrick's Day parties), not to mention the many groups organized by the Carlton churches. Plays, like "Uncle Tom's Cabin," "Ten Nights in a Barroom," and C.S. Primrose's "A Prince of Sweden," were performed at the Carlton Opera House and the Cloquet Symphony played at the Village Hall. In the summer, circuses would arrive. Kit Carson's Buffalo Ranch Wild West and Trained Animal Exhibition, featuring the reenactment of "The

Grooming was always important. The Halliday Barbershop started in 1880 and is pictured here in the 1920s. Ruth Halliday, wife of Harry Halliday and daughter-in-law of Tom Halliday, was one of several women who have served as barbers in Carlton. This shop later became the Williams Barbershop and does business today as the Powers Barbershop. Photo courtesy of Darold Powers

Battle of Wounded Knee," was performed in July of 1911. In June 1916, the Chautauqua, with all its singing and inspirational talks, came to town for five days. Baseball teams were organized each year and their fortunes were followed by enthusiastic fans. The Fourth of July celebrations, with parades, bands, speeches, and games, were an annual high point. During the winter basketball was beginning to make its appearance and hockey was played on the mill pond at Otter Creek.

The Carlton Rebekah Lodge in the 1920s. First row: Mrs. Clark, Mrs. Anna Swanson, Mrs. Alma Froberg, Mrs. Ethel Swanson. Second row: Mrs. Emily O'Donnell, Mrs. Flossie McFarland, Mrs. Ruth Cain, Mrs. Marie Baumann, Mrs. Christenson, Mrs. Jeannie Thompson, Miss Bernice Johnson, Mrs. Olive Walton. Third row: Mrs. Ella Schultz, Mrs. Ina Williams, Miss Frances Waugh.

Bert Hassing up to bat! Baseball was a major summer activity that was followed enthusiastically by the whole community. Here the son of the *Vidette* owners gets his innings in during the summer of 1931.

The Carlton City Band in the 1920s. The city band was an important element of both entertainment and culture in any community in the world before widely available and portable recorded music. The band would always play at parades and community events, but it would also hold regular concerts on summer evenings.

Chub Lake was available for picnickers and campers, as well as for the cottage owners. J.B. Thomson ran the pavilion and picnic area and rented about ten boats. The *Vidette* estimated that on one glorious Sunday, July 28, 1917, there were about 500 people at the lake. In fact, beginning in the summer of 1914 the Carlton Commercial Club organized a town picnic at the lake. The stores closed for a day in August, people were to bring their own lunch, and coffee and lemonade were supplied by the merchants. Games and contests were organized, prizes were given, and it was deemed a success. The *Vidette* claimed proudly, "It won't be many years before Chub Lake will be one of the best summer resorts in the northwest." Nevertheless, Lake Carlton, or Lake Ogontz (as it was called by the Great Northern Water Power Company) or the Thomson Reservoir, as it is now known, had its supporters too. As early as 1907 the *Vidette* wrote about the beauty of the lake's islands and their suitability for picnics. In August 1915 the paper reported that A.M. ("Si") Brower had launched a power boat on the Lake Carlton and was getting "deadheads" out of the water, with plans to make an attractive beach and swimming area. Carlton did not lack for entertainment.

"It's summer time, and the living is easy." Chub Lake was close enough to be a very convenient place for Carlton, Thomson, and Wrenshall people to come for picnics, Sunday outings, and summer cottages. People also came from as far away as Cloquet, Duluth, and Superior. Photo courtesy of Barbara Gravelle

"Gone fishin." Howard Sheils, Ed Watson, and Ralph Flaugh have brought back some trophy fish from Chub Lake.

With all of this building and the physical improvements to the town, with the provision of water and sewer, electricity and telephones, surfaced streets and roads, concrete sidewalks and street lights, and businesses, Carlton emerged by the early twentieth century as a modern community. The town had taken much of the shape that it has retained to this day, but still expansion was underway. By 1912 the Woodland Park area north of Walnut Avenue had opened up and lots were being sold by A.D. Haish of the Carlton Improvement Company, and W.M. Cain had a surveyor laying out lots west of town. In March of 1910 the Village Council had struck a committee made up of C.H. Shaver, W.M. Cain, and D.C. Anderson to devise a way of reviving the fortunes of the town. It seems to have worked. On October 8, 1911, the *Vidette* printed the headlines, "Carlton is on a Boom these Days." As the county seat, with a strong industrial base, and placed in a key location, Carlton had truly come of age.

Sources:
Beck, Bill. *Northern Lights: An Illustrated History of Minnesota Power.* Duluth: Minnesota Power, 1985. Pp. 143-58 .
Carlton County Vidette, February 24, 1964.
Haubner, Maurice. *Pillars of Society.* Privately printed, 1983. P. 13.
Ledgers of the Secretary of the Carlton Village Council, Carlton County Historical Society.
Stillwater Gazette, cited in Minnesota Federal Writer's Project, M529, Roll 134, MHS.

Nellie Barnard

Nellie Evelyn Barnard was born on December 12, 1862, to Augustus H. and Catherine Smith Barnard of Indiana. Little is known of her youth, but she came from Kansas to Carlton as a young woman of twenty-four to work as a bookkeeper for Captain James M. Paine in 1886 and remained for forty-two years. As the bookkeeper for the Paine interests, Miss Barnard came to know all of the employees in the sawmill, the lumber camps, and the other Paine enterprises.

Nellie Barnard, a remarkable business woman in early twentieth century Carlton.

When Captain Paine died in 1900, and his lumber operations closed, Miss Barnard succeeded him as the head of the Carlton County Abstract and Title Company and she served as manager of the extensive Paine estate. She also ran the Carlton Stock Farm, south of town, and the Carlton Horse Market. The Horse Market was a highly successful enterprise drawing customers from all over the region. It dealt with a variety of animals but specialized in large work horses commonly used in lumber camps. When the large barn housing the horses and market burned in 1914 it was only partially covered by insurance. Nevertheless, Miss Barnard was able to rebuild by spring of that year and to pay off all of her debts. As a farmer, Miss Barnard specialized in pure-bred Guernsey cattle and became, first, Secretary and, in 1917, Vice President of the Northeastern Guernsey Breeders Association. "Many people believe that this is a business for men only, but they are mistaken," she said. "Women in this business can be as successful as men." In all of her areas of competitive commercial endeavor she emerged as a highly successful business woman.

Miss Barnard was also very much occupied in the community life of Carlton, taking a particularly active role for many years in the Carlton Study Club and the Carlton School Board. She was a member of the J.M. Paine Presbyterian Church, where among other things she taught Sunday school. Miss Barnard died on September 7, 1928, of liver cancer, and she was given a large funeral where members of her Sunday school class sang one of the anthems.

Carlton County Vidette, April 20, 1917, and September 13, 1928

The Carlton Horse Market. The crowd attending the auction gives some idea of how popular and successful the Market was.

James Dunphy

James Dunphy was born in Guelph, Ontario, on May 17, 1860, to Mr. and Mrs. Stephen Dunphy. After his mother died when he was still an infant, he was put out to be raised by friends. At nineteen he left for the United States, staying briefly in Michigan, and in 1885 arriving in Northern Pacific Junction to join his father, who ran the Trading Post and Stage Stop at what is now Scotts Corner, and his uncle, John Dunphy, who had homesteaded near Hay Lake and witnessed the Northern Pacific sod turning ceremony on February 15, 1870. One of the remarkable elements of Dunphy's life was the multitude of jobs that he held in pioneer Carlton County. His first work was with the St. Paul & Duluth Railroad building bridges and culverts, he cut timber in the area, he worked as a storekeeper and a builder, and finally ran a hotel in Carlton. In 1892 he started "The Big Store," which sold a vast array of merchandise, from small trinkets to farm machinery. Dunphy also extended credit to people who were attempting to get started in Carlton or at farming. In so doing he helped numerous people get their feet on the ground and lead productive lives. Dunphy was regarded as a very shrewd businessman and a good judge of character, and he claimed to have made several fortunes. But he also had bad luck. In 1911 two of his ten children, Pearl, aged 11, and Florence, aged 13, drowned while at a picnic at Chub Lake, and in 1913 his first wife, Lydia Haubner died. In January 1917, "The Big Store," which was only partially insured, burned to the ground. Family members and several people living in the building barely escaped in their night clothes.

One of the pioneers of the Carlton community. Dunphy worked at a number of trades in Carlton's early days, but he was remembered for running the "Big Store," a general store that seemed to sell something of everything until it was destroyed by fire. Dunphy then ran successfully for County Treasurer. After he retired he wrote his colorful memoirs for the *Vidette*.

Dunphy chose not to rebuild. Instead, he ran for County Treasurer, an office to which he was re-elected four times. When he retired on May 17, 1940, at eighty-four, a celebration was organized by his friends. In 1937 and 1938 he wrote his memoirs for the *Carlton County Vidette*, which provided a vivid personal glimpse into the life of early Carlton and a description of a very large number of early settlers. Dunphy lived to the age of eighty-four, retaining a keen mind, keeping active, and walking several miles every day. He died suddenly of a heart attack on June 11, 1944, in his house in Carlton.

Carlton County Vidette, June 15, 1944.

NOTICE

All public meetings are forbidden in the Village of Carlton for an indefinite period, as a

Preventative Measure

until the outbreak of Spanish Influenza has abated.

By Order of the Village Council

Carlton, Minn., Oct. 30.

CHAPTER 8

War and Depression
Twentieth Century Troubles

Historians like to say that the twentieth century really began with the outbreak in 1914 of World War I, or the Great War, as it was originally called. As a result of the Great Depression, World War II, and the Cold War, with all of their conflicts, war and crisis came to characterize the twentieth century. What is so striking about these events is the degree to which they touched everyone in the society and the extent to which they also changed that society.

When the United States entered the war in 1917 Carlton was plunged right in, as was the rest of the county. The coming of the war could not actually be seen as a surprise, the *Vidette* having reported on the crisis in Europe since the assassination of the Austrian archduke, the subsequent battles across the continent, and the challenge the German submarine policy presented to the United States. As early as October of 1914, the First National Bank was accepting contributions to provide relief for war victims in Europe, and on August 15, 1916, Cordelia Paine and her sister, Mme. Blandin, organized a "preparedness dance" at the pavilion at Chub Lake, "preparedness" being a popular movement to push the government to get the United States on a war footing. As the ominous headlines in the *Vidette* traced the deterioration of American relations with Germany, the paper urged women to join the Red Cross society and to help with recruiting. Congress declared war on Germany on April 6, 1917, but for local people war came

on April 17th when a soldier on the Thomson dam, already under Army protection, challenged four men who had stopped their car and had climbed onto the dam. When they did not respond the soldier fired his rifle in the air. The intruders fired back, fled back to their car, and headed for Duluth. There was no evidence as to who the men might have been, but it was suspected that they were members of the radical labor union, the International Workers of the World, who opposed the war. The *Vidette* reported, "Shooting opened Tuesday" and worried about spies and aliens and complained that "all our moves are known to the enemy." By mid-summer the Minnesota Home Guard replaced the Army in patrolling the Thomson dam and power station.

World War I called for public service from all walks and ranks. Organizations like the Boy Scouts were well placed to step forward to be helpful and patriotic. In this parade the Boy Scouts in full uniform march behind the flag.

Many young Carlton men enlisted right away, such as S.J. Searls, who became a cavalry officer, and Wilson Gillespie, Oscar Nicholson, William Lane, Ed Karnowski, Clarence Armstrong, Ernest Magnuson, John Lynch, and Lief Larson, all of whom joined the Marines. The United States, however, implemented the draft almost immediately. By June 6th, 1917, all young men between the ages of 21 and 30 were ordered to register, in Carlton at the Village Hall, and near the end of July the first draft calls were announced. Although postponed several times, the first train loaded with 82 Carlton and area boys left for Camp Dodge, in Des Moines, Iowa, on the 22nd of September. They were hosted at a dinner the night before and the Cloquet band played as they boarded the train. A second train-load of young draftees was sent off in late December. Carlton was now really in the war.

The home front was immediately involved in the war also. Cordelia Paine and her sister, Mme. Blandin, who came home from New York in the summer of 1917, began organizing the Red Cross society in Carlton. They arranged space in the school on Monday, June 4th, for women to make surgical supplies and dressings. "Every woman who has the time to spare to devote to this work should make it a point to be present on that occasion," Miss Paine said. "There's always something doing for the good of the community when Miss Cordelia and her sister are on the job," the *Vidette* observed approvingly. There were no officers for the Red Cross society, but Mrs. Guy C. Smith was put in charge of membership and the number of women who participated was very large. Money for the society was raised by a benefit concert at the Carlton Public Library. The Carlton efforts received praise from Ann Morgan, the daughter of the late J.P. Morgan, on behalf of the American Society for French

Some four million eight hundred thousand men served in the U.S. armed forces during World War I, of which almost four million were in the Army. John Lynch looks like one happy soldier.

Many local boys served in the armed forces during the war. Young Melvin "Curly" Oien served in both the Army and the Marine Corps. Oien is shown here while a Marine on board ship with the fleet.

World War I required the mobilization of the country on a scale unlike anything in the United States since the Civil War. The Red Cross provided an opportunity for civilians, particularly women, to make a valuable contribution to the war effort. Here the Carlton women's Red Cross Bandage Making Class is on parade.

Wounded of New York. In addition to Red Cross work, there was plenty for people to do to discourage hoarding and to help sell Liberty Loan bonds to finance the war. Patriotism was also stirred in the Carlton Opera House by a showing of "The Birth of a Nation," one of the most powerful motion pictures of the day.

Carlton was not without its casualties in the Great War. Oscar Nicholson had been one of the first to volunteer for the Marines. In June the *Vidette* had published two of his letters home, in which he said that he was "getting along fine" and that the war at the front was "not much trouble so far." On the 18th of July, 1918, he was dead. Nicholson served in the Fifth Regiment at the Second Battle of the Marne, Belleau Wood, and Soissons. Vern J. Brower and George McFall, two Marines, were also wounded at the Marne. Albert Sellgren served in the 30th Division of the U.S. Infantry. He was killed during an assault on the Hindenburg Line on October 17, 1918. Lieutenant Spencer J. Searls, the bright young Carlton lawyer and member of the legislature, was hit by shell fragments that killed several soldiers near him, though badly wounded he survived.

OSCAR NICHOLSON ON THE GREAT ROLL

MAKES SUPREME SACRIFICE FOR HIS NATIVE COUNTRY

KILLED IN ACTION JULY 18

MESSAGE FROM WAR DEPARTMENT WEDNESDAY, CONVEYS NEWS

Carlton County Vidette,
September 6, 1918.

The end of the war was overshadowed in Carlton and the rest of the region by the great 1918 fire that destroyed Cloquet, Moose Lake, and several other towns and killed at least 453 people, injured many more and drove thousands out of their homes. Even the draft calls were suspended in the aftermath of the fire. Carlton was spared destruction, probably because the area north of town which had been burned two weeks before served as something of a barrier. But people streamed into Carlton by train, by car, and on foot seeking shelter on the night of October 12th. People of Carlton opened up their homes and gave generously of whatever they could to assist their neighbors who had become refugees. The Odd Fellows Hall and even the Courthouse sheltered people. Cloquet *Pine Knot* editor Orlo B. Elfes heard his name called as he and his wife and daughter sat huddled in the relief train in the Carlton station, having just left the burning city. It was stationmaster Lee Brower inviting them to stay with his family. Young Maurice Haubner drove his father's car into Carlton and took a dozen refugees back to the family farm near Scotts Corner.

The great fires of 1918 drove large numbers of refugees into Carlton. Within a matter of hours, Red Cross, the National Guard, and the Minnesota Home Guard were in place to deal with the crisis. Photo - MHS

Mrs. Henry Oldenburg described to her daughter Margaret, teaching school in Coleraine, the scene with as many as fifty people taking shelter in their house—the McNairs, the Hornbys, the Coys, the Schlenks, the Walters, the Flemings, and more. She said fire burned between the Great Northern and Northern Pacific tracks, near the McCausland farm. After the fire Cloquet and Moose Lake people stayed in Carlton and the area for months as their homes and towns were rebuilt. The Hornby family took over the Paine house, Stonecroft; the Weyerhaeusers moved out to their summer home at Chub Lake; the *Vidette* and the *Pine Knot* published combined editions; and so on. The discussion to rebuild Cloquet took place in the Oldenburg house and the *Vidette* promised, "Cloquet is Rising from its Ashes." Peace and "normalcy" came back to Carlton only very slowly in 1919.

Improved roads constituted a major project for the community after the war. County roads had been built gradually since the early settlement in the 1870s and before. The Military Road had been the first, and a branch of it had been extended from Twin Lakes to the St. Louis River. Similarly a road from Thomson to Carlton had been built, more or less paralleling the railroad. In 1882 a road was built west and south to Barnum and Moose Lake and the following year a road north to Cloquet as well. These were all rough dirt roads, very muddy after rain or snow, and most unsuitable for the growing number of automobiles and trucks. The Carlton County Good Road Association lobbied the County Commissioners from early in the century. Beginning in 1919, Carlton ben-

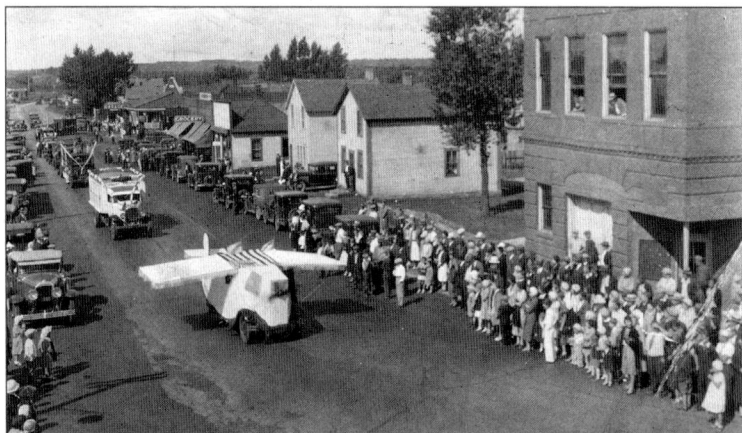

Floats in a parade along Chestnut Street in 1932. The old Village Hall is on the right.

efited from the state program to develop something of a modern road system. State Highway Number 1 was to enter Carlton from the west, proceed through the town, turning north toward Scanlon, Cloquet, and Duluth. Carlton citizens were eventually able to persuade the state to run the highway into Carlton along Chestnut Street, turning north on Third Street, past the new courthouse. Work was started in 1920 and completed in September of 1924. (This became Highway 61 in 1934.) While the work was being done building the highway, the major streets in Carlton also were paved, making for a much neater looking community. Several other roads were up-graded during the 1920s. The old road to Thomson was improved in 1924 to provide access to Jay Cooke State Park. That road eventually became State Highway 210. Improvements were similarly made to the west as far as Cromwell in 1924. That same year the county roads south from Carlton to Wrenshall, Twin Lakes, and Blackhoof were also worked on and improved.

With the building of the highway along Chestnut Street, the "main street" in

Carlton shifted north. It was a harbinger of what the twentieth century would hold. In the nineteenth century the railroad had been king, and naturally in Carlton the "main street," North Street, faced the tracks. Throughout the latter part of the twentieth century the automobile was king, a point that the people of Carlton recognized immediately. Several of the businesses on North Street were jacked up and turned around to face Chestnut Street, where the action would be. Those buildings that were too large to be turned around (the Walters building) were simply moved from North Street straight back to the sidewalk on Chestnut Street, their old pressed tin facades still visible from the south.

Several major institutional buildings remained to be constructed to bring Carlton into the twentieth century. Another major structure in the town was the county courthouse. A two and a half story red brick courthouse had been built in 1890, but it was no longer adequate as the county grew in size, now almost twenty thousand, and more services were needed. In 1920 plans were drawn by the Minneapolis architect, Clyde M. Kelly, for a three-story stone structure in a Classical Renaissance Revival style

The new courthouse rises. The open-topped segmental pediments are in place over the doors, as are the brick pilasters with Ionic capitals on the second and third stories.

and the cornerstone was laid in November 1922. This dignified building is faced with Indiana limestone and brick and has massive pilasters of Bedford stone. The halls feature beautiful interiors made of creamy white Kasota marble, with black Belgian marble trim, terrazzo, and oak. The ceiling in the main hall has oak beams and several of the offices and chambers have oak wainscoting. The new courthouse was opened with a dignified ceremony on February 22, 1924, with speeches by former State Senator Fred Vibert of Cloquet, Henry C. Oldenburg of Carlton, and Judge Bert Fesler, the District Judge, architect Kelly, and several others; music and prayers were also provided. The building cost about $250,000 and was paid off by February 1943. The courthouse has provided important facilities for the county offices, District Court chambers, and a number of other public facilities. As Maurice Haubner said, "People from every part

Work began on the new courthouse in late 1922. It cost the county $250,000 which was paid off in twenty years. Built of brick and Bedford stone, the courthouse was also reinforced with steel girders.

of the county sooner or later visit the courthouse," and the Carlton County Courthouse is one in which every citizen can take pride.

The new Carlton County Courthouse was completed in early 1924. Its opening was celebrated by speeches, music, and prayers. Built in the Classical Renaissance Revival style, the courthouse has remained a dignified location for county government.

The original Carlton Village Hall, a wood frame structure, was built in 1881, and an addition had been constructed two years later to provide for a jail and a jury room. In 1904 a bond issue was approved to raise $5,000 to build a new Village Hall. This was a two-story brick structure that included meeting facilities and a small jail. It was located at the corner of Chestnut and Third Streets. However, the building obstructed the view of automobile drivers passing through Carlton on State Highway 61 who needed to make a right angle turn at the corner. In 1936 the state condemned the Village Hall and tore it down so that the space could be opened up and the corner rounded. A new Carlton Community Building was built a half a block away on Chestnut Street at a cost of $50,000 by the Works Progress Administration, one of the New Deal relief agencies that attempted to fight the Great Depression. Outcroppings of rock on Chestnut Street were also blasted away, expanding the road to a uniform width. Another New Deal agency was the Federal Writers' Program which published *Minnesota: A State Guide* in 1938 and *The Minnesota Arrowhead Country* in 1941. These books sketched automobile tours for parts of

The new Carlton Civic Center on Chestnut Street replaced the old Town Hall in July 1937.

Minnesota and provided descriptions of the principal towns and sights along each tour. In the first book Carlton was described as a "town, almost surrounded by wooded hills and prosperous dairy farms," but its interest was its proximity to Jay Cooke State Park. *The Minnesota Arrowhead Country* gave a good brief history of Carlton, telling the story of the building of the Northern Pacific and the struggle to become the county seat. "The village throve, with lumbering and railroading, its chief industries," the guidebook wrote, and "When lumbering began to decline, agriculture superseded it." The book also gave a flattering description of the Carlton school, the new courthouse, and the new community building.

The Great Depression of the 1930s fell across the land just as powerfully as the war had done. In the aftermath of the 1929 stock market crash, the national economy slowed and refused to recover. This caused untold economic distress to millions of American families. Among other things, it pushed both men and boys out of their homes to search for work. Hitching rides on freight trains was the typical means of transportation for the unemployed in those days. Carlton being a major railroad junction had large numbers of men passing through the rail yards, living in the hobo camp west of town, and often getting into trouble in the process. When the administration of President Franklin D. Roosevelt came into office in 1933, it immediately began a series of programs designed to employ people and discourage the aimless wandering. The Civilian Conservation Corps (CCC) was designed specifically to rescue young men, get them off the streets, feed them properly, give them some practical job training, and provide them with some income (they were paid $30.00 a month, of which $22.00 was sent home to their families). Some 1,500 camps were built all across the United States, organized by the Army, and under the supervision of local people; roughly two million young men between the ages

Originally called the "River Inn," the Refectory, which is now called River Inn Visitors Center, at Jay Cooke State Park is one of the lasting legacies of the work of the CCC in the area.

of 17 and 23 were put to work on various conservation projects. Two CCC Camps were built in Carlton County, one at Big Lake and one at Jay Cooke State Park, near Forbay Lake. Camp SP-2 was started in June of 1933, bringing in 189 young men from Kansas under the command of Major Jack H. Hood of Fort Leavenworth. A barracks and dining hall were started immediately and were ready by September, and work in the Park was undertaken in the autumn, including an entrance gate. The Camp ran until October of 1935 when a number of Camps were consolidated. The Camp at Jay Cooke was reopened in May of 1939 as SP-21, Company 2711, and continued in operation until May of 1942, when the whole CCC program was closed down. Most of the 200 young men recruited for this Jay Cooke State Park Camp were from Carlton County. They were put to work improving the road through the Park, clearing out the hiking trails, planting trees, fighting forest fires, setting up picnic sites, constructing tourist cabins, and rebuilding the Swinging Bridge (which lasted until the floods of 1950). Their legacy, however, was the building of the several magnificent stone and log structures: the River Inn refectory, near the Swinging Bridge, and the facilities at Oldenburg Point. They were taught skills and trades that would eventually help them find employment and were given an opportunity to finish high school. The young men of the CCC also made an impact in Carlton, spending their earnings in local stores, making possible the re-opening of the Park movie theater, and holding dances, open houses, and entertainments. The Civilian Conservation Corps has been remembered fondly by both the public and its former members.

Life went on during the Great Depression, although through various means. For example, the federal government abandoned the experiment of Prohibition, repealing the Volstead Act and the Eighteenth Amendment to the Constitution in 1933. The Carlton County electorate reversed their decision of 1915 and voted for liquor. The Carlton Village Council received applications for licenses to sell "non-intoxicating malt liquors" by April from Joseph Zacher, Jr., Marion Anderson, Axel Elfstrom, the King and Wing Café, Mrs. K. McFall, the National Tea Company, John Newquist, and A.E. Cable; and full liquor licenses were sought as soon as the Amendment to the Constitution went through. Neither the town nor the county exercised the option to remain dry, but Carlton was never altogether comfortable with the resumption of the sale of alcohol. One way to partially control the use of

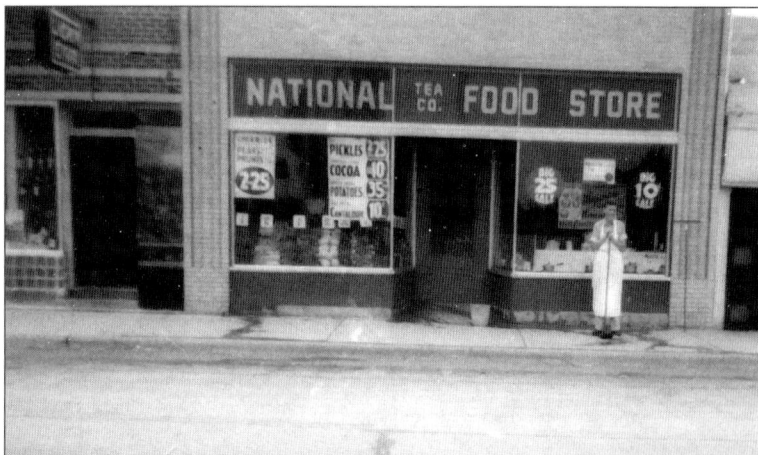

The National Tea Food Store on Chestnut Street. The original building collapsed into the excavations for the Street Car Café next door. This is the rebuilt store. Della Smith was manager from 1927 to 1941.   Photo courtesy of Barb Schmidt

alcohol was to sell it through a Municipal Liquor Store, and in 1939 the Carlton Liquor Store was created. A decade later the store was given the authority to serve drinks as well, and it operated until 1982.

Sporting events served as a diversion as well as a source of civic pride in the Great Depression as well as today. The 1930s saw Carlton achieve some considerable success under the leadership of the outstanding local athlete, Harry Newby. Originally from

The Carlton basketball team did exceptionally well in the 1930s under the leadership of coach Harry Newby, shown here with one of his teams. Back row: Harry Newby, Harry Gillespie, Bob Anderson, Jim Gillespie, Roy Anderson, Harry Lawrence, Bill Holsworth, and George Roley. Front row: Jim McIntire, Don Harper, Clayton Oswald, Verne Brower, Wesley McIntire, and Bill Harper.
Photo courtesy of Bob Anderson

Tamarack, Newby had been a brilliant athlete at St. Olaf College, and as a professional football player, being featured twice in Robert Ripley's syndicated newspaper column, "Believe it or Not." In 1935 Newby was hired to coach football, basketball, track, and baseball at the Carlton High School (he also taught biology, social science, and physical education for both boys and girls and led a Boy Scout Troop). While baseball and football were very popular sports in the community, Newby had exceptional success with the school basketball teams. In March 1937 he steered the Carlton Bulldogs to victory in the District 26 Championships, defeating Cloquet by 20 to 18. Again in 1939, Carlton won the District title, edging out Proctor 25 to 23. "Carls show great poise, stamina, and ability," the *Vidette* reported proudly. The town celebrated. Newby left Carlton in 1939 to coach in Thief River Falls, before serving in the Navy during World War II. After the war he returned to Carlton as Register of Deeds, although he lived in Cloquet.

The economic crisis caused by the Depression made many commercial ventures difficult or impossible. To deal with the matter of bank failures across the country the Roosevelt administration declared a national "bank holiday" and refused to let banks reopen until they had satisfied government requirements. The First National Bank of Carlton was required to raise $45,000 of additional capital before it could reopen, but through the energetic efforts of A.B. (Bert) Loban, then a farmer, that sum was exceeded in five days. The bank only made two foreclosures during this difficult period. It took some courage to make financial commitments dependent on future business in those years. In 1934 young Dr. Maurice H. Haubner, the local boy now returned as the town dentist, began construction on a handsome, two-story, brick

John Duffy Motors and Reed's Drive-In.
Photo courtesy of Mike Duffy

office and apartment building on Third Street, the largest building project of the decade. Although the financing was precarious, by 1936 the building was complete and occupied by Haubner himself, Dr. Wingquist, a physician, Clarion Williams, a barber, Fred Kennedy's meat market, the Zacher brothers' liquor store, and two apartments on the second floor. A later building project was the construction of John Duffy's art-deco garage, filling station, and restaurant, completed in 1941. Selling Skelly gas, this new drive-in provided twenty-four hour service with the restaurant specializing in soda pop and ice cream. Both of these projects employed the skills of Carlton builders and craftsmen.

Farmers protest on the steps of the courthouse in 1937. Economic hardships during the Great Depression led to protests, demonstrations, work stoppages, and strikes across the country, and Carlton County was not immune.
Photo by Acme Newspictures, Inc. - MHS

The Great Depression caused economic distress that was felt in Carlton and the region. Farms across the county labored under difficulties with market prices, mortgages, loans for seeds, and relief of one kind or another. Nevertheless both the number of farms and the amount of acreage under cultivation in the county grew between 1930 and 1935. Retail business suffered, and many people were unemployed. The two railroads reduced the number of trains operated through Carlton, both limiting service and diminishing their workforce. By 1934 the *Vidette* reported that there were 2,542 men and 85 women registered for relief work in Carlton County. Labor unrest was generated by these conditions. Even the WPA workers went on strike briefly. In January 1937 some 4,000 lumberjacks and forest workers went on strike, bringing much of the forest industry to a halt. The strikers not only walked off the job in the woods, but they also blocked major roads, like Highway 61 at Scanlon, obstructing easy movement in northeastern Minnesota. While negotiations went on for months, not surprisingly bad feelings developed between the strikers and the industry, and also between the strikers and many small farmers who worked as timber producers. Major violence was avoided and a final settlement was reached in November 1937.

Even before the effects of the Great Depression were over the impact of World War II was upon the United States. International tension and war had been building in Europe and Asia since 1930. When hostilities broke out in Europe in September of 1939, the United States again declared its neutrality. For the most part the *Vidette* was not focused on the war in Europe, although it gave quite good coverage of the Russo-Finnish War, including reports of local fund raising and relief activities on behalf of Finland. However, after the fall of France in 1940 the crisis took on a new urgency for the coun-

Crown Prince Olaf and Crown Princess Märtha of Norway stopped in Carlton on their tour of the United States in 1939. Margalo Sather of Scanlon presented them with flowers.

try. In the course of the next twelve months the United States began providing assistance to Great Britain, China, and later the Soviet Union, through the sale of munitions, the Destroyer-for-Bases agreement, and Lend-Lease. In October 1940 the government put in place the first peace-time draft in an attempt to get the Army on something of a war footing. The first names were drawn by lot on October 24th. Thus, when the Japanese attack on Pearl Harbor plunged the United States into the war in December 1941 some important steps had already been taken. Renewed appeals were made in February 1942 for men between the ages of 20 and 45 to register for the draft, and by October the age limit for registration had been lowered to 18. On March 5th some forty young men from Carlton and the surrounding area were sent off to Fort Snelling to be inducted into the Army. Further draft calls were made every two months. The *Vidette* reported the news about local boys in the service. A Carlton young man, Second Lieutenant Vern Neil, completed pilot training at Stockton Field, California, and got his wings; Richard L. (Dick) Bugbee entered flight school at the

Ben E. Johnson in uniform, with Mogan McClay and "Gop" Waugh.   Photo courtesy of Tim Johnson

Naval Air Station at Pensacola, Florida; James L. (Pete) Lee was promoted to Major in the Army Air Corps (by October he made Lieutenant Colonel); Private Dwight M. (Monte) Brower saw the President and General George C. Marshall at a parade at Kelly Field, San Antonio (he was later given a commission and became a pilot); Navy Lieutenant Robert Evans was home on furlough after service at Guadalcanal (he was later reported missing in the South Pacific). Casualties were noted as early as July of 1942: John Rayner, serving on the *USS Pillsbury*, was reported miss-

A death of someone in the service was made known and remembered in the community by a small flag with a gold star that was hung in the window of the person's family. These Gold Star Mothers, Mrs. Lindberg, Mrs. Stine, and Mrs. Holsworth, had given up their sons for the nation.

ing in action; in 1943 Raymond Hopp, who was from New Ulm but lived and worked in Carlton, was killed in North Africa; Lieutenant Harold A. Watkins, was also killed in North Africa; and Marine Corporal Frank R. Stine and Marine Private First Class Alfred LeRoy Lindberg were reported killed in the South Pacific. By the end of 1943 casualties were reported with increasing regularity.

The war also made itself felt on the homefront immediately. By February 1942 sugar and rubber automobile tires were rationed, imported goods like coffee, tea, and cocoa, as well as other food products soon followed. The Red Cross mounted big campaigns for support, enlisted women to make bandages, and appealed for donations of blood. The government organized large War Bond Drives right up to December 1945. By January 29th 1942, air raid wardens had been appointed; John H. Duckstad was chief observer and his assistants were Forest B. Piper and Harland Harper. Air raid drills were held from time to time and lights were blacked out at night. On March 19, 1942, the *Vidette* asked the question, "Can an enemy force stage a blitzkrieg and bomb our local dam and railroad bridges, manufacturing plants, canal entrance to Duluth harbor, electric plants and wire systems?" and concluded, "Certainly, they can." To prevent such an attack, the road through Jay Cooke State Park was closed beyond Oldenburg Point and soldiers guarded the Thomson dam and the power stations along the St. Louis River, as they had in 1917 and 1918. All kinds of activities were seen to be part of the war effort. "Cutting Pulp Wood is YOUR Fight," ran one advertisement in the *Vidette*, but other campaigns, such as scrap metal drives and waste paper drives encouraged the participation of young and old in the community. Grace D. Christenson from Carlton served with the Red Cross in India, and Captain Kathryn Kavanaugh served as an Army nurse. The war was omnipresent: the Park movie theater showed a steady selection of war films in its weekly menu—films such as *Wake Island, One of Our Aircraft is Missing*, and *Army Surgeon*. The *Vidette* serialized the classic story of PT Boats, W.L. White's *They Were Expendable*. It was, therefore, with almost inexpressible joy and relief that on August 16, 1945, the *Vidette* published the headlines: "WORLD DELIRIOUS WITH PEACE."

World War II was brought home to everyone in America by the process of rationing goods needed for the war effort or scarce goods shipped in from overseas. Many scarce commodities were collected and reused by the war industries, such as scrap iron, copper, paper, and old automobile tires. Here tires could be collected at McCausland's Texaco Station.

The war is over!

World War II Veterans Plaque given to the community by the Carlton Business Women's Club in 1943. The top row, designated by a star, were casualties of the war.

Sources:

Benson, David R. *Stories in Log and Stone: The Legacy of the New Deal in Minnesota State Parks*. St. Paul: Minnesota Department of Natural Resources, 2002.

Carlton County Vidette, 1914-1945, quotations from May 11 and June 1, 1917, June 7, 1918, October 25, 1918, March 19, 1942, and August 16, 1945.

Carroll, Francis M., and Franklin R. Raiter. *The Fires of Autumn: The Cloquet-Moose Lake Disaster of 1918*. St. Paul: Minnesota Historical Society Press, 1990. Pp. 51-52 and 181-83.

Haubner, Mauice H. *Pillars of Society*. Privately printed, 1983. Pp. 30-31.

Ledgers of the Secretary of the Carlton Village Council, Carlton County Historical Society.

Mitchell, Stacy. "Union in the North Woods: The Timber Strikes of 1937," *Minnesota History*, vol. 56, no. 5 (Spring, 1999).

Nelson, Edward, and Barbara Sommer (eds.). *It Was a Good Deal: The Civilian Conservation Corps in Minnesota*. Duluth: St. Louis County Historical Society, 1987.

Oldenburg, Mrs. Henry, to Margaret Oldenburg, ca. October, 1918, Henry C. Oldenburg Papers, Minnesota Historical Society.

Skalko, Christine, and Marlene Wisuri. *Fire Storm: The Great Fires of 1918*. Cloquet: Carlton County Historical Society, 2003. Pp. 37-38 and 125.

The WPA Guide to Minnesota, with an introduction by Frederick Manfred. St. Paul: Minnesota Historical Society Press, 1985. P. 293.

The WPA Guide to the Minnesota Arrowhead Country, with an introduction by Francis M. Carroll. St. Paul: Minnesota Historical Society Press, 1988. Pp. 90-91.

Dr. Maurice H. Haubner

Maurice (Mike) Haubner was born in 1906 in Carlton to John and Katherine (Peacha) Haubner. Haubner's family and experience embodied much of the history of early Carlton and Carlton County. His mother's family, the Peachas, were of French-Canadian and Irish extraction and had settled in Minnesota in the 1860s and farmed and worked in the lumber trade. His father was of German ancestry and came from Elgin, Ontario, following other members of his family to Carlton. His aunt's marriage to James Dunphy linked him to that pioneer family. His father worked in French-Canadian lumber camps, a saloon, a boarding house, and a livery stable. Young Haubner's childhood was filled with images of a frontier town, filled with saloons, lumberjacks, railroad men, immigrants, and Indians. There was swimming in Otter Creek, skating on the millpond, magnificent Fourth of July celebrations, and the antics of drunks to keep him amused. However, after their house in Carlton near where the water

Dr. Maurice H. "Mike" Haubner
dentist and civic leader.
Photo by Robert Pue Photography,
courtesy of Michael Haubner

tower is now located burned to the ground, one of three disastrous fires the family suffered, they moved to Hay Lake. There John Haubner built a temporary shack and attempted to farm. His father seemed good hearted and well intentioned but unlucky and a poor provider. Young Mike remembered always being cold and hungry, but in this setting he learned to fish and hunt for food. During the great 1918 Cloquet fire he brought refugees to his parents' home in the family car.

Haubner had attended school in Carlton from first to fifth grade, but now living in the country the ten year old Mike went to the Lone Pine School and the McKinley School. His return to Carlton was the result of an inquiry by the school principal to his father as to whether he would attend high school. The principal arranged for him to earn his board and room while living with the Gust Moser family, south of town. Impressed by his father's sister who was a dentist, Haubner determined to get training in dentistry. After graduating from high school, Haubner spent a year at Superior State Normal School and worked before entering the University of Minnesota Dental School in Minneapolis. Although he had to support himself with odd jobs, selling woolen goods door to door, and working nights in a mortuary, Haubner graduated in 1929 and returned to Carlton. He acquired the practice of two dentists who had not been able to make a living, but by dint of working nights and weekends he was able to earn an increasingly good living. He introduced an X-ray machine and anesthetic gases, and developed great skills in working with gold and silver and the making of dentures. In 1933 he married Marie Lessard and together they raised three sons, Dr. John, Phillip, and Dr. Michael.

Dr. Haubner had both a keen business sense and a strong public spirit. Having barely got his practice started in the depths of the Great Depression, he committed himself to building a large two-story brick office complex on Third Street, which was completed by 1936. He then built a substantial new house for his family in Woodland Park. He later converted the family home at Hay Lake into apartments. Once World War II was over he became the driving force in the effort to build a community hospital in Carlton, and he put a substantial amount of his own money into building the walls of the structure. The project languished, however, to be revived in the form of the Carlton Nursing Home in the mid-1950s. That enterprise was successfully completed in 1955 with Dr. Haubner as president. Dr. Haubner was also active in several dental associations, a charter member of the Carlton County Sportsmen's Club, and a member of St. Francis Catholic Church. He had been a keen hunter and fisherman since childhood, and he enjoyed travel both in the United States and abroad. He died on July 16, 1998, in the Carlton Nursing Home he had done so much to create.

Haubner, Maurice H. *Pillars of Society*. Privately printed, 1983.
The Pine Knot, July 18, 1998.

The Haubner family home near the courthouse in Carlton. This house burned, prompting their move to Twin Lakes. Would the infant be Maurice Haubner?

Crime!

The notion persists that crime and violence are features of modern life and represent a decline from the more idyllic and rural world from which we have descended—a world in which everyone knew and trusted each other, left their doors unlocked, and walked the streets and country roads confidently and without fear. A reading of the *Carlton County Vidette* would soon reveal just the opposite to be the case. Its pages are filled, week after week, with alarming stories of break-ins, stick-ups, bank robberies, shootings, and from time to time murders. In June 1907 the office of C.H. Shaver in Carlton was broken into, but the attempt to open the safe failed. In August there was a successful robbery in Thomson. In November 1916 robbers broke into the back window of the First National Bank of Carlton, but while attempting to manipulate the combination lock on the safe they set off the alarm bell. The clanging noise roused the cashier, Guy C. Smith, and many citizens, but the robbers managed to flee. Some ascribed this criminal activity to hobos or drifters who made their way to Carlton on the railroads, often wandered through the town begging, and had a hobo camp outside of town. Others felt that liquor and saloons were the source of moral degradation that ruined peoples' lives, destroyed their ability to make an honest living, and led them into criminal activities. A new brick county jail was built in 1914, next to the courthouse, and clearly it was well used.

On September 29, 1920, about midnight, two masked men held up the Carlton train depot at gun point, taking twenty-four dollars from the Stationmaster A.M. Brower's cash box and an undisclosed amount from the waiting passengers. Several people were threatened and one beaten on the head, causing him to bleed extensively. The robbers then fled out onto the street where they jumped on the running boards of a passing car driven by Bob Anderson (of the Anderson Store), who was forced to drive the desperadoes first to Duluth and then across the bridge to Superior, where he too was robbed and left with only fifty cents for the toll to get back across the bridge. After a robbery spree in central Wisconsin the two men took the train to Cloquet. They were seen stashing a sack on Dunlap Island by two inquisitive boys who upon investigation discovered their revolvers, among other things. The boys quickly told Police Chief John McSweeney about the weapons and McSweeney was able to make the arrest and return the two men to Carlton for trial.

One spectacular incident that transcended most petty crime took place in Carlton on Wednesday, June 17, 1931; this incident might be called "The Shoot Out at the King and Wing Café." Early that morning Sheriff Selmer W. Swanson was informed of a robbery in Cromwell in which a Ford run-about had been used as the get-away car. Finding a car of that model outside the café run by Bessie R. King and N.H. Wing, Sheriff Swanson got his deputy, A.W. Beatty, and constable, Bert McFarland, and entered the café to arrest the suspects while they were having their coffee. During the attempted arrest one of the robbers pulled a gun and began shooting. Constable McFarland was hit in the arm and the abdomen and a patron in the restaurant was hit in the face. As the two robbers fled, the Sheriff shot one of them in the arm. The wounded robber escaped out the back door and fled toward Thomson, past the Oldenburg house, trailing blood. The other armed bandit ran upstairs above the café and hid under a bed, where he was subsequently captured. The Sheriff then sent out a bulletin to other law enforcement officials in the region, with the result that shortly after noon the wounded robber was discovered in Jay Cooke State Park near the power station, where he surrendered without offering further resistance. A third man in the café with the robbers turned

Scene of the crime—the King & Wing Café pictured after the shootout. Emil Luukkonen is behind the counter. He owned the café in the 1930s after he had served a term as Carlton County sheriff. Photo by Olson Studio courtesy of Larry Luukkonen

out to be a hitch-hiker who had been given the ride of his life. The patron in the café who was shot was a drifter from Superior and was an innocent victim. He died in the Raiter Hospital in Cloquet that evening. Constable McFarland, although shot twice, went first to the Post Office to say that he could not deliver mail on his route that morning, before being taken to the hospital. He survived. The bullet holes in the wall of the King and Wing Café became part of Carlton folklore.

In November 1941 Sheriff Louis Schiedermayer asked Clara Holm, the owner of the Carlton Motor Company, to help identify the kind of car that had been used in a bank robbery in Moose Lake. Although there was some confusion about the color, the car was finally identified as a cream colored, 1941 Chevrolet cabriolet. On Thanksgiving Day, while driving along Grand Avenue in Duluth with her mother on their way to a family dinner, Miss Holm was passed by a car of that description, driven rather recklessly by a young man. Miss Holm speeded up and followed the car off Grand Avenue toward the Patrick Duluth Knitting Mill. There she made a note of the street address where the car was now parked and the license number. She was later able to tell the Sheriff the address and number of the car she had seen. The Duluth police were informed and they investigated. The man in question had recently paid off his debts and was leaving for Louisville, Kentucky. However, when confronted, he confessed. Miss Holm's tip led to the arrest.

Clara Holm—Carlton businesswoman, Chamber of Commerce president, and heroine of the 1941 bank robbery.
Photo by Guy C. Caldwell

Carlton County Vidette, 1 and 8 October, 1920, and 4 December 1941.
Carol Beckstrom, "Nostalgia," Carlton County Historical Society.
Larry Luukkonen, "High Noon at the King & Wing Café," Carlton County Historical Society.

Always ready for a party. Big crowds at the August 1954 Carlton Barbeque Jubilee, celebrating the opening of the new Carlton to Wrenshall highway.

CHAPTER 9

Happy Days
Twentieth Century Boom Times

The world of post-war America was different from that of the earlier part of the century. World War I had brought the United States onto the world stage but only temporarily, the "Roaring Twenties" generated a kind of prosperity, and the Great Depression had created an economic crisis that shook the confidence of Americans. World War II had engaged the country like nothing since the Civil War and in a variety of ways it seemed to have changed almost everything. The United States was now unavoidably the leading world power, which brought new and often unwelcome responsibilities through the United Nations, the Cold War, the outbreak of war in Korea, the Vietnam conflict, and so on. Economically, the United States was also at a high point, untouched by the kind of physical destruction that the war had inflicted on Europe and Asia and revitalized after the insecurity of the Great Depression. The war and the booming economy broke down barriers and changed the social and cultural world of Americans. On the one hand, the Cold War and the worry over a possible nuclear conflict generated public attention on civil defense and committed a generation to service in the armed forces. On the other hand, the yearning for domesticity that the sacrifice of war had stimulated emerged by the 1950s as an emphasis on youth and on material conveniences—most notably household appliances and the automobile. All of this is often remembered today through the images of the popular television show, "Happy Days."

In Carlton the tremendous focus on the war, on the soldiers and sailors, on war work, rationing, and the sale of War Bonds, receded very slowly. Soldiers and sailors were steadily discharged and returned home throughout 1945 and 1946. In June 1946 the *Vidette* reported that over 2,000 Carlton County men and women had been discharged from the service. The G.I. Bill of Rights gave them access to benefits that provided low interest loans to buy homes and start businesses or pay for training or education. A Veterans of Foreign Wars Post was organized in 1935 (named after Nicholson and Sellgren, the two Carlton soldiers killed early in World

The Carlton Veterans of Foreign Wars was organized in the 1930s, and in 1945 this club was opened. The building had been a hotel before becoming the VFW club.   Photo courtesy of Barb Schmidt

War I), but the social needs of these newly returning service people were met by the opening of a VFW Club in 1945 in the old McFall Café where friends could get together. When this wood frame building burned in March 1952 the Post was able to take over a brick building on Second Street.

World War II and service in the military was a powerful influence on what we now call "The Greatest Generation." The Veterans of Foreign Wars and the American Legion were the organizations that enabled the "Vets" to share their experiences, look after each other, recognize the sacrifices they and their comrades had made, and keep alive something of the spirit that motivated them during the war. As years passed, veterans were given full military honors when they died.

Gradually other matters caught the public eye. A polio epidemic in the summer of 1946 spread suffering and fear in the region. With no vaccine then available, the Carlton County Fair was cancelled, along with the Minnesota State Fair and numerous other summer events, in order to help reduce the danger of exposure from large crowds of people. The opening of the Carlton School was pushed back to September 9th, although several other area schools waited until the 16th. The activities of the Carlton High School and the PTA, sports teams, 4-H Clubs, Boy Scouts, Keep Minnesota

Before the vaccines and serums were developed by the end of the 1950s, poliomyelitis, or infantile paralysis as it was also called, was a terrible scourge. Children were particularly vulnerable, but adults were not immune either. Summer was "polio season," and every year children were struck with the disease. Some recovered with no effects, some were crippled for life or even confined to an "iron lung" to enable them to breathe, and some died. No one seemed to know what caused it. Getting chilled? Mingling in crowds? Going to the circus? Eating green "polio" apples? It was a source of great anxiety.

Green meetings, the Goodfellowship Club, civic affairs, and car accidents increasingly occupied Carlton people. And especially the weather! In June of 1946 tornadoes ripped through Barnum, Moose Lake, and the region, causing extensive damage. Four houses and forty-one barns were destroyed; four people were injured and seventy-five families affected. The Red Cross had to be called in. In February of 1948 the worst blizzard in twenty-five years paralyzed the region. Winds of fifty to sixty miles an hour drove the snow into drifts twelve feet high. Cars were stalled along Highway 61 and events in Carlton on the 27th and 28th were cancelled. When summer came there was no rain. By autumn of 1948 there was the worst forest fire danger in twenty years and even

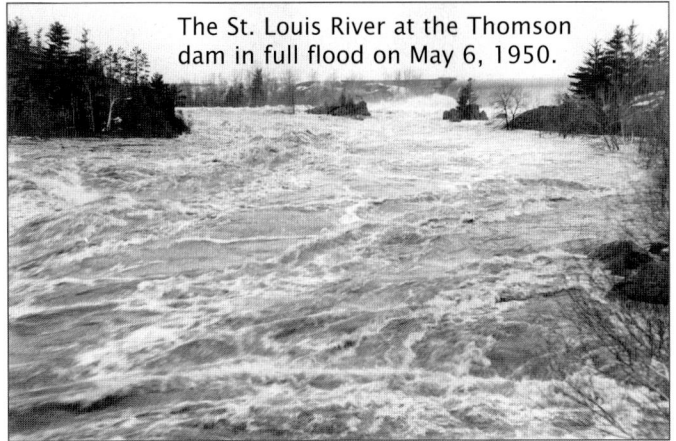

The St. Louis River at the Thomson dam in full flood on May 6, 1950.

Minnesota Power and Light Co. worried about power shortages. A year and a half later, in the spring of 1950 the St. Louis River and Otter Creek were higher than they had been in years. Carlton only suffered water in basements, but there was extensive flooding in Cloquet and Thomson and the Swinging Bridge at Jay Cooke Park was washed out. People said all of this extreme weather was caused by the testing of nuclear bombs. No one at this time had heard of Global Warming.

Carlton held several large celebrations over the decade, largely organized by the Commercial Club. The first was the Carlton Jubilee Celebration held on September 4 through 6, 1948. The town was filled with activities and entertainments. There were street dances, square dances, an auction, races and games for children, horse racing and amateur boxing for adults, a baseball game featuring the House of David Club versus the home team, and carnival rides. Over the course of several days some 35,000 people lined the streets for the magnificent parades and to hear Governor Luther W. Youngdahl, Mayor of Minneapolis Hubert H. Humphrey, and Senator Joseph H. Ball. Miss Nona Harper was made Jubilee Queen and Paul Bunyan, King of the Northland, presided over it all. The following summer Carlton joined in the celebrations for the centennial of the formation of the Minnesota Territory in 1849. The Commercial Club, reorganized in March

In September of 1948 Carlton held its Jubilee Celebration. This included several days of parades, carnivals, games, speakers, and street dances.
Photo courtesy of Darold Powers

as the Carlton Chamber of Commerce, planned another three-day celebration on August 12 to 14, 1949. A program of street dances and games and races was put together once again, with Cedric Adams, a popular Minneapolis radio personality, as the main attraction. Five years later the first Carlton Barbeque Jubilee was held on August 6th and 7th, 1954, celebrating the opening of the new Carlton to Wrenshall highway. There were rides, concessions, a band concert, street dances, and speeches by U.S. Senate candidate, Val Bjornson. This event, the first of many called the Barbeque Jubilee, was really the beginning of Carlton Daze. The Centennial of Carlton County was celebrated three years later, 1957. Delegations from across the county traveled by bus to the state capitol to promote the event, and over the course of the summer there were pageants and celebrations in several towns in the county. Carlton's celebration took place on May 23rd. President Dwight D. Eisenhower was invited but was unable to attend. A large parade was followed by the burying of a time capsule in the courthouse lawn. Lists of community officials from around the county, together with samples of various items produced in the county were placed in the capsule. The celebration was climaxed by a smorgasbord dinner. It should be kept in mind that these special events were held in addition to the annual Memorial Day, Fourth of July, and Labor Day celebrations, with parades, and

On May 23, 1957, a time capsule was buried in the court-house lawn, as part of the celebration of the Carlton County Centennial. The time capsule included a list of community officials from around the county and examples of the various products manufactured in the county. Speeches were made, the band played, and the artifacts were preserved for posterity.

often rides and concessions. During these years the region was particularly rich in accomplished high school marching bands and American Legion drum and bugle corps, to which was added, in 1952, the extremely popular Carlton Clown Band. There was no shortage of summer entertainment for the Carlton community in these "Happy Days."

The somber note during this time was the outbreak of war in Korea in June 1950 and its implications at home and abroad. The Cold War reached one of its periodic crises, bringing the country to a war footing. The *Vidette* carried a weekly column of "Service Notes," telling of the postings and promotions of local men and women in the service, and usually there were some special stories on the front page as well. By September 1953, when an armistice had been signed and most of the casualties were over, the *Vidette* reported that eleven Carlton County men had been killed in action, three had died of wounds, three had died of accidents in the U.S., one had drowned in Korea, and three had been held as prisoners of war. There had been 775 county men in the service since 1950, of which 350 had been discharged at that time. The most dramatic and touching story was that of that of John L.

The service took Carlton boys around the world. Navy Lieutenant Junior Grade John A. Watkins in Japan in 1951.

(Jack) Thornton, from Barnum, who had been blinded and badly wounded by a grenade. Thornton, cheerful and positive, returned a hero and was feted by 450 people at a dinner in his honor in the Carlton School gymnasium on April 12, 1953. The Carlton American Legion named its post after Thornton. A year and a half later he became engaged to Joyce Campbell, a Cloquet woman who had lost her sight at age 13 as a result of a snowball accident. Money was raised to help them settle in a house in Cloquet, and the Wood Conversion Company, where Thornton had worked before going into the Army, remade a machine that he could operate by sound signals. They were married in the St. Francis of Assisi Church in Carlton on September 25, 1954.

A National Guard unit was organized in Carlton in 1948 and drilled in the Civic Building, although it was merged with the Guard unit in Cloquet when a new Armory was built there. The exercises and activities of the National Guard, as well as the annual summer camp, involved many local men, and were well reported in the local paper. Civilians too participated in Civil Defense activities and exercises. A watch tower was set up on top of the Civic Building. Carlton acquired a Civil Defense Rescue Truck in 1954 and in 1956 large exercises were held in Carlton, including a Skywatch program that trained plane spotters.

Btry A 257th AAA Gn. Bn.
Captain R. J. Nagorski
Camp Ripley, Minnesota

In addition to meeting locally once a week, the men in the National Guard went off each year to summer camp. Here, under the command of Captain R.J. Nagorski, the Minnesota guardsmen from Carlton are shown at Camp Ripley following their fifteen day training exercise in June of 1952.
Photo by Gordon Guy, courtesy of Ben Anderson

Related to the defense of a community is the question of its health. In the years after the war Carlton went through a prolonged process to create a suitable and affordable health care facility. Public discussion first emerged as early as July of 1946. Carlton had doctors and maternity facilities from its earliest days, but no general hospital.

Inspired by Dr. Maurice H. Haubner, construction started on the Carlton Hospital in 1948, but money for the project ran out and the building stood for years as an empty shell. By the mid-1950s the hospital project was reorganized as a public corporation and refocused as the Carlton Rest Home. Shares were sold, money was borrowed, and work resumed. Leonard Wilson, Ruth Finberg, Dr. Maurice H. Haubner, and Dave Hanson, check the plans.

Pushed by the town dentist, Dr. Maurice H. Haubner, and the new physician, Dr. John K. Butler, the Commercial Club took up the idea on April 15, 1947, and organized a dance and a keno party to raise the money to make a feasibility study. Roughly a year later, with a favorable report, a decision was made to build a community hospital, 100 feet by 37 feet with a capacity of 25 to 30 beds, some three blocks north of the courthouse. A non-profit organization was put together and began construction after getting approval from the Minnesota Board of Health in 1949. Unfortunately, it was not able to raise enough money to complete the project, with the result that for several years the half-finished building languished. Drastic changes were required. In June of 1954, with the advice of Carlton lawyer Leonard A. Wilson, the hospital organization was changed to a public corporation which could sell shares and borrow money. The purpose was changed from a community hospital to a seniors home. The money was raised, largely by Dr. Haubner and Bert Loban, and work resumed. On May 8, 1955, the Carlton Community Nursing Home was opened to the public; Dr. Haubner was president of the corporation and Loban, formerly president of the First National Bank, was the Resident Manager. The first patients moved into the 22 bedrooms and three wards roughly a week and a half later. It was the beginning of what would be an extensive seniors complex in Carlton.

By 1955 the new Carlton Rest Home was completed and opened for residents. Photo courtesy of Norman Johnson

The engine that drives a community is often its business and commerce, and Carlton had a thriving commercial life. On September 19, 1947, the *Vidette* claimed that Carlton was enjoying a "New Building Boom." Work had started on the two-story com-

munity hospital; Karl Stuckenburg had purchased an old pool hall, demolished it, and was constructing a one-story brick building for his restaurant; Clara Holm was remodeling part of the Carlton Motor Company facility; Duane Johnson was building a structure that would be a mortuary and furniture store on one level and apartments above; and various new homes were being built in the residential areas. Carlton already had a lumber yard, a municipal liquor store, several car dealers and service stations, several grocery stores (soon to be called supermarkets), a wide selection of restaurants and cafes, the O.F. Walters general merchandise and clothing store, and the Park Theater. In

Karl Stuckenberg's Café became a popular eating spot in Carlton for over thirty years. Young Julius Stuckenberg prepares his meats in the kitchen.

1950 Delbert (Deb) Oien opened the Carlton Appliance Company and five years later he moved it into the Walters building, which was shared for several years. O.F. Walters' store operated in Carlton for over fifty years; when it was finally closed Deb Oien was able to take over the entire building and make his store into one of the largest appliance dealerships in the county. Bill and Dwight Kortie of Cloquet opened the Gamble Store in Carlton in 1955 and Sylvester Schafter remodeled and expanded his jewelry store as well.

The Carlton economy, and that of the region, was given a dramatic boost by the development of the oil industry in the area. In 1950 the Lakehead Pipe Line Company completed an extensive pipeline that brought crude oil from Canada to Superior, Wisconsin. This line ran underground, south of Carlton near Chub Lake. The following summer the International Refineries Company announced that it would build a $7,000,000 oil refining facility at Wrenshall on the site of the old brickyards. By October 1953 the refinery was dedicated and operating. It had a capacity of producing 11,500 bar-

The International Refineries in Wrenshall brought new technology and new jobs to the region. This large facility operated from 1953 to 1981.   Photo by Powers Studio

rels a day of gasoline, fuel oil, heating oil, and industrial fuel oils (later expanded to 16,000 barrels), which were distributed throughout Minnesota and Wisconsin. The company employed over one hundred and fifty people and had a payroll of $70,000 a month. Indirectly it gave work to additional large numbers of people, such as truck drivers, and thus made a powerful impact on the local area. There were difficulties, however. The refinery seemed to have persistently bad labor relations and strikes were a problem from the very beginning. There was hardly an environmental movement in those days, but even so there were worries that the refinery's dumping of wastes into Silver Creek would ruin one of the finest trout streams in the region.

Expanding Carlton into what became South Terrace was a major commitment for the community, with the building of houses, roads, schools and infrastructure. The sod breaking ceremony took place on April 19th, 1953. This was a big investment, but by the mid-1950s the first houses were completed.

To take advantage of the refinery in Wrenshall and the growing economy in the region, in 1951 Carlton began expanding its boundaries south of town into what became known as South Terrace and the Webbeking Addition. It was planned that 800 acres of new territory would be brought within the town limits, and a corporation was created to build houses in the addition with the refinery itself becoming a major shareholder. The project got FHA approved financing in 1952 and ground breaking took place on Sunday, April 19, 1953. South Terrace, Inc. was able to show its first model homes in the summer of 1957—they were the four bedroom, split-level *Brookline* and the three bedroom, full basement *Troy*. These were modern, up-to-date houses which required water and sewer facilities and access to good roads. Carlton was confronted with the need to up-grade its infrastructure to handle this kind of expansion. A bond issue was passed to borrow $95,000 for the up-grading of the water and sewer system, but it meant that the town would have an ongoing financial obligation. The old bridge over Otter Creek and the road south from Fourth Street were seen to be inadequate

Part of the upgrading of the infrastructure of Carlton involved improving the water system. Here is the filtrations plant for taking iron and other minerals and substances out of the water.
Photo courtesy of Carlton City Clerk's Office

for the heavy oil trucks coming out of the refinery, so a whole new road extending to Wrenshall south from Third Street was constructed, along with a new bridge over Otter Creek. This work was completed by the summer of 1954.

Carlton was pulled to the west as well as to the south in these years also. The building of Highway 33 in the late 1940s from Cloquet to the junction of Highways 61 and 210, near the site of the early gravel excavations created something of a north/south/east/west hub. The Olson's Motel and a popular restaurant run by Everett Olson created the beginnings of a settlement still known as "Olsonville." These circumstances took on a new complexion on December 19, 1957, when the state highway authorities announced plans to construct a new interstate highway along the route of much of the existing Highway 61. However, the new interstate would bypass Carlton and

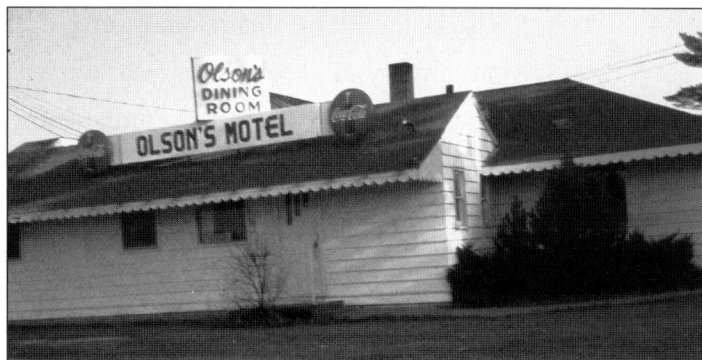

Olson's Motel and Dining Room gave a name to the growing western area of Carlton on Highway 210.
Photo courtesy of Tim Johnson

the existing route through the town, and extend from the junction of Highways 61, 210, and 33, in a gentle arc to the new bridge being built across the St. Louis River at Scanlon. "This might seem like a death blow to Carlton business," the *Vidette* noted, "but with a little foresight much can still be gained." The paper concluded that Jay Cooke State Park would still draw tourists from the interstate and that they would have to drive through Carlton. In the long run, the Interstate system would have a profound effect on America and particularly the rural communities. In the immediate local situation, the *Vidette* was confident that Carlton would rise to the challenge.

The Interstate system brought the world of the combustion engine to full flower and accelerated the decline of the old railroad system that by the end of the 1950s was becoming visible to all. The great pre-World War I plan to make Carlton a major terminal for the Northern Pacific Railroad was never realized, but Carlton remained very much a railroad town during the subsequent decades. Certainly freight traffic remained high, with iron ore, coal, and grain cars rolling through Carlton on both the Northern Pacific and Great Northern lines.

The last regularly scheduled Northern Pacific passenger service through Carlton was this single diesel powered "Budd Car" from Staples to Duluth. It carried a few passengers, luggage, and mail. Its last run was on May 25th, 1969. The building to the left was the Carlton depot and the Great Northern switch tower can be seen in the distance.   Photo by John Blamey

Train wrecks were still a spectacular diversion, occurring from time to time. Many of the derailments were quickly reversed, but periodically there were major collisions. In one such case, in June of 1951, a Milwaukee freight ran into a Northern Pacific train west of Carlton. The brakeman on the Northern Pacific train was killed and many cars were destroyed. When the railroads converted from steam powered locomotives to diesel engines Carlton lost its coal sheds, water tower, and in April 1959 its engine house. The last working steam locomotive of the Northern Pacific system went through Carlton on January 17, 1958. The railroads were changing fast; however, it was passenger service that suffered from the competition of cars and buses. In 1954 there were still eight Northern Pacific passenger trains a day stopping at Carlton. The president of the railroad was scolded by the chairman of the Minnesota Railroad and Warehouse Commission and told that the train station had been inspected and was found to be in very poor condition, but the gross earnings of the station were satisfactory and justified a new station, and that the modern town of Carlton deserved better service. President Robert S. Macfarlane replied that the station was "admittedly in rather poor condition and rebuilding would be desirable," but other work had been given priority and the budget was already committed. In fact, rather than improving the service the response was to cancel two of the Duluth to St. Paul passenger-mail trains in early 1958. Over the next decade all of the old passenger trains were removed from service. The last passenger train that operated through Carlton was the Northern Pacific's "Budd Car" (named after the president of the company), a single railcar for passengers, powered by twin diesel engines, running between Staples and Duluth. This was cancelled on May 25, 1969. The Great Northern had terminated its passenger service through Carlton sometime earlier.

Carlton had its origins in the building of the Northern Pacific Railroad, so the one hundredth anniversary of the railroad was a cause for meaningful celebration in the town. Town leaders, the governor, rail club enthusiasts, and a few Northern Pacific executives attended the celebrations and a dinner in the South Terrace School on February 15, 1970. A large sign was set up near Highway 210 showing where construction had started in 1870. Carlton civic leaders and visiting dignitaries had their pictures taken at the spot. Govenor Harold LeVander is taking a turn with the shovel. Ironically, three weeks later the Northern Pacific disappeared into the new Burlington Northern Railroad.

AT THIS POINT
ON FEBRUARY 15, 1870
THE CONSTRUCTION OF THE
NORTHERN PACIFIC RAILROAD
WAS COMMENCED

Nevertheless, as 1970 approached, people in Carlton wanted to commemorate their link with the Northern Pacific. A Centennial Dinner was organized at the new South Terrace School on February 15, 1970. Ed J. Kavanaugh, the president of the Chamber of Commerce was the master of ceremonies, and there was a long list of distinguished guests, headed by Governor and Mrs. Harold LeVander and Wayne Purcell, Chairman of the Carlton County Board of Commissioners. Neal Nickerson of the Carlton County Historical Society gave the welcome, Frank Young of the St. Louis County Historical Society the response, Governor LeVander made a few remarks, and Don King, General Manager of the Eastern Lines, Northern Pacific, gave the main address of the evening. Wayne Olsen, a well known railroad enthusiast and photography collector, provided the entertainment in the form of a slide show of pictures of the early Northern Pacific. It was a wonderful evening, celebrating the one hundred years of the railroad that had built Carlton and many of the towns and cities across the northern states. Three weeks later the Northern Pacific ceased to exist. The Northern Pacific, the Great Northern and the Chicago, Burlington & Quincy were merged into the new Burlington Northern Railroad.

Stanley Gilpin gets his commemorative ticket punched by Conductor Ernest Oakes.

It was the end of an era.

Sources:

Carlton County Vidette, 1945 to 1970, quotations from December 19, 1957.

Haubner, Maurice. *Pillars of Society*. Privately printed, 1983. Pp. 32-33.

Ledgers of the Secretary of the Village Council, Carlton County Historical Society.

Northern Pacific Papers, Presidents' File, 137.D.15.5 (B), File 950, Oliver A. Ossanna (Railroad and Warehouse Commission) to Robert S. Macfarlane (President of the Northern Pacific), March 15, 1954, and Macfarlane to Ossanna, April 15, 1954; and Advertising, File No. A-88 (i), NP Centennial, 134.H.10.4 (F), Minnesota Historical Society Collections.

Boy Scouts provided a wonderful organization through which to channel the energy and enthusiasm of adolescent boys into activities that were service oriented, educational, and physically demanding. The camping, woodcraft, and canoeing programs were particularly suitable for northern Minnesota boys, plus there were countless other skills and adventures to be pursued through the scouts. The Boy Scout Court of Honor was the ceremony in which the boys were promoted in rank and awarded the merit badges they had earned. The ceremonies taught ritual, traditions, and dignity. Here the scouts of Carlton Troop 177, Errol Niemi, Greg Oien, John Roley, Lloyd Schleicher, Jim Councilman, and Jim Zimmerman, have lit the ceremonial candles representing the principles of the Boy Scout Oath and Law.
Photo courtesy of Linda Newlon

Two members of the Carlton Chamber of Commerce, meeting at Stuckenburg's Café in 1952. Ray Butts, on left, and Ed Kavanaugh with Mrs. Butts and Mrs. Marge Kavanaugh.

For a number of years the Carlton County Historical Society Museum and Library was in Carlton, downstairs in the Haubner building. Then as now, the Historical Society organized numerous events, such as this sleigh ride. In the driver's seat are Charles Dahlberg, and Mrs. Ordelia Smith; in the center, Mrs. Jewell Anderson and Dr. Maurice H. Haubner; and in the back seat, Nancy Finberg and Mr. and Mrs. Gordon Aanerud, the owners of the team of Belgian horses being held by Brett Aanerud.
Photo by Denny's Studio

In January of 1974 dog sled races were held in Carlton at Chub Lake. Celebrities, such as Duluth broadcaster Marsh Nelson, came to participate. The winners went on to further competition in Ely. Photo courtesy of Ron Johnson

Bowling became very popular after World War II. Men's and women's teams were organized, but families and groups could play just for fun. This Carlton women's team included Elaine Soderberg, Helen Newquist, Evelyn Dancer, Gladys Wills (holding the ball), Delphi Oswell, and Angie Wavren.
Photo courtesy of
Donna Melin

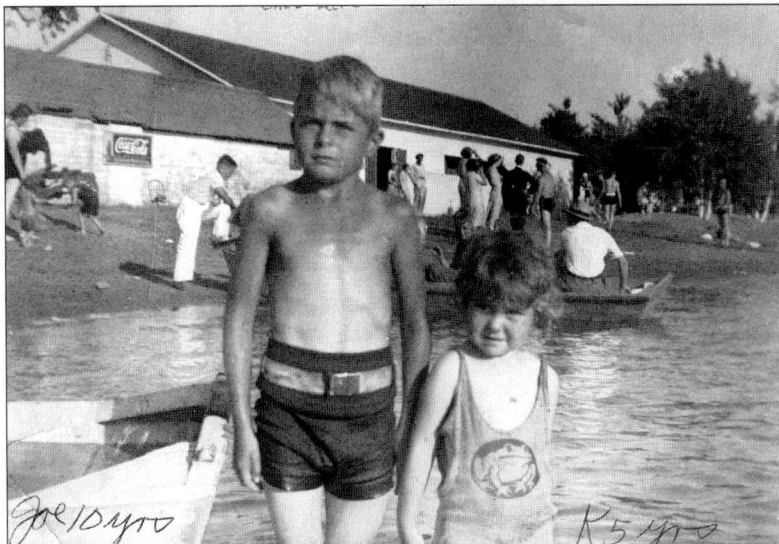

Summer at Chub Lake. Joe and his little sister Kay Lavigne are in the water in front of the old pavilion at Chub Lake. Besides swimming, boats could be rented for fishing or one could get snacks in the pavilion. Photo courtesy of
Kay Vigliaturo

1959 Basketball

In 1959 excitement rose as the Carlton Bulldogs went to the Minnesota State Basketball Tournament where they placed #2 in the state.

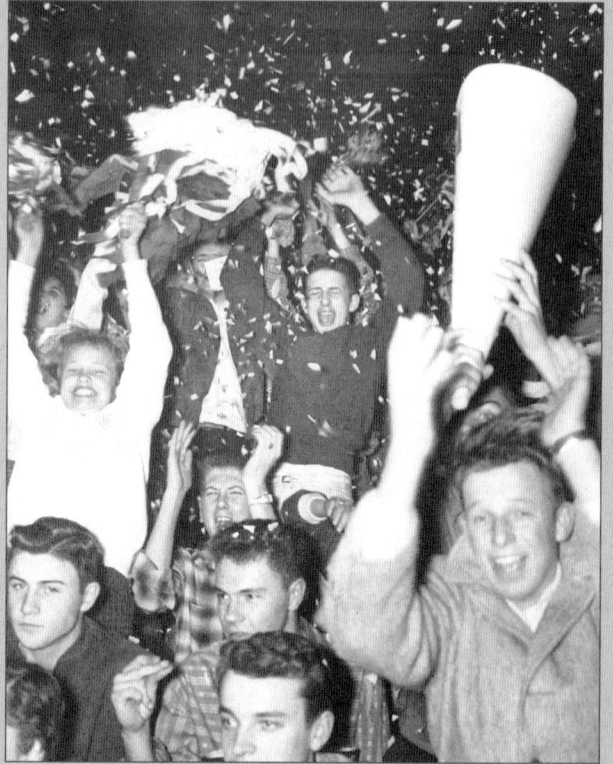

Carlton is awarded the trophy for winning second place in the 1959 State Basketball Tournament. Receiving the trophy are Fred North, John Pierson, and Dennis Bjork. Photos by Charles Curtis

Team members follow the game—Doug Anderson, Roger Skelton, John Pierson, Dennis Bence, manager, and kneeling, Fred North. Cheerleaders Karen Rystrom, Carolyn Ahrens, Beverly Mesto, Phyllis Munter, Beverly Collins, and Marion Koch, watch anxiously.

Charlotte Zacher

Charlotte Zacher was born in Carlton in 1912, one of six children, to Joseph and Ada Zacher, German and Swedish immigrants who lived in a tar-paper shack on the edge of town. She was drawn into the restaurant business while she was still attending Carlton High School. Her brothers, Jim, Joe, Jr., and Les, bought a railway car for seventy-five dollars in 1928 and moved it to a lot on Third Street where they opened a twenty-four hour diner, the Street Car Café. Charlotte trained for two years as a school teacher at the Duluth State Teachers College with her sisters, Ellen and Rose, but she concluded she was not a teacher. She worked in the diner serving ice cream cones and coffee for five cents and hamburgers for ten cents. A brick building replaced the old railcar, and a bar was added downstairs. The excavation for the downstairs lounge led to the spectacular collapse of the National Tea Store next door on October 20, 1937. (The National Tea Co. opened the next day in an empty store across the street.) Charlotte would run down to serve beer for five cents a glass and then back upstairs to pour coffee. When her brothers went into the service Charlotte took over the restaurant, the rental of the six motel rooms, and paid off the mortgage. The Street Car Café became Charlotte's Restaurant and Motel and developed a loyal clientele over the years. At work by five in the morning, Charlotte did all her own cooking as well as serving the customers on the eleven stools and in the two booths.

Charlotte Zacher and Dolly Johnson pose at a familiar Carlton landmark.

Charlotte had always liked dancing and getting dressed up, and looking back on her life thought she might have become an actress. Sometime in the 1970s she began wearing her formal dresses and jewelry while serving her customers, especially on holidays. Soon long gowns and frilly lace, often in pink, or shorts and boots, became Charlotte's trade marks. Charlotte became something of a celebrity in Carlton, grand marshal of a parade, featured on the national television show *Real People*, as well as local TV and newspapers. Charlotte ran her restaurant right into her eighties and her birthdays were regularly celebrated by her loyal fans. After over sixty years in the business, Charlotte and her restaurant became an institution in Carlton. She brought a touch of kindness, color, and humor into the lives of many people in Carlton and the whole region.

Charlotte Zacher at a dressup occasion at the café.

133

The Carlton Fire Department

Carlton, like all frontier towns, was particularly vulnerable to fire throughout its early history. The combination of wooden buildings, wood or coal fired heating systems, oil lamps for lighting, and individual pumps for water supplies, meant that almost every building was at risk and no adequate fire fighting protection could be deployed. The great fire of 1900 that destroyed most of South Street, the several schoolhouse fires, and the regular household fires, seemed to illustrate the point that something needed to be done. A volunteer fire brigade was formed and permission was obtained to hook hoses to the Northern Pacific's water tank, but these were only partial gestures.

The Carlton Fire Department responded to a fire in a building that was located behind the high school.

Even the promise to deliver water to all parts of the town through the construction of Carlton's own water system was not the complete answer. The disastrous fire that destroyed James Dunphy's "Big Store" in January 1917 drove home the limitations of the fire brigade as it then existed. In April of 1934, fire started in the Lee Lumber Company warehouse and, driven by a strong south wind, soon got into a shed and stacks of 75,000 feet of lumber. The fire brigade was quickly on the scene, but was unable to make any progress against these extreme conditions. The fire spread to other buildings and the town was again threatened. Fire departments were called from Cloquet and West Duluth and also a detachment of CCC boys from the Jay Cooke Park camp came to assist. Altogether some two hundred people fought the fire before it was brought under control. As the *Vidette* periodically pointed out, disasters like this illustrated the need for a well organized and well equipped fire department.

Although there were in Carlton hose carts and pumps and volunteers that can be traced back to the beginning of the century, and a new Chevrolet truck with Laverne equipment that was acquired in 1936, the

Firemen Harry Lee, Don Reed, George Metke, Maurice Nordstrom, Ed Turcotte, and Everett Froberg pose with Engine # 3 in the mid 1950s.   Photo by Denny's Studio

founding of the modern Carlton Fire Department wasn't seen until 1939. A Chief and Assistant Chiefs were appointed, a roster of crews of between 20 and 25 men were made up (with a waiting list for new members), and twice-a-month training was given to teach the crews how to handle their equipment and how to deal with different kinds of fires. Gradually better, newer, and more sophisticated fire trucks and equipment were acquired. An ambulance was added in 1968 and the "Jaws of Life" in 1981. Agreements were also worked out with other communities for cooperation and assistance when crises arose. In the late 1980s the Fire Department was moved out of the Civic Building, with its exit on North Avenue to a large new Fire Hall on Fourth Street. Today the Carlton Fire Department has two pumper trucks, a tanker, a grass fire rig, and two ambulances. Its regular territory includes, not only Carlton, but also Thomson and Twin Lakes and Sawyer Townships.

The Fire Department does a demonstration to the delight of a large crowd at their garage behind the city hall.
Photo courtesy of Donna Melin

Firemen from 1997 stand at the ready—front row, l to r: Wayne Johnson, Darold Powers, Dave Anderson, Daryl Nyquist, Walter Anderson, Elmer Berg, Francis Roy, Robert Clark, Sylvester Isaacson, back row: Millard Crandall, Bob Rubesh, Stuart Beck, Merle Waller, Charles Schmidt, LeRoy Baker, Mick Balow, Bert Whelan, Sylvester Schafter.   Photo courtesy of Darold Powers

The Carlton Feed Mill, one of the oldest businesses in the community, provides the backdrop for the new park and the paved paths of the Willard Munger State Trail which is used by hikers and walkers to access the beauty of the area.

Photo by Tim Johnson

CHAPTER 10

Epilogue: A New Day

The last years of the twentieth century were not easy for the United States and for its small towns and rural communities, and the first five years of the new century seemed to offer an even greater challenge. Many of the large retail stores that formed the center of the commercial life of these communities gave way to the shopping malls and big box stores of nearby cities. For some towns and villages this was the end of the road. Carlton needed to reinvent itself. The population, which had declined in 1950 to 650, went up again in 1960 to 862 and reached a high point in 1970 at 884. During the 1980s and 1990s the population declined slightly and in the 2000 census was reported as 810. However, what should be kept in mind is the "suburbanization" of much of the rural countryside surrounding Carlton. The pool of people living around Carlton and utilizing the resources and facilities of the town had continued to grow. It was in these circumstances that in 1974 Carlton's incorporation was changed from a village to a city, thereby qualifying it for both state and federal assistance.

Carlton celebrated its centennial in a four day holiday from July 23rd through 26th, 1981. Earlier Kim Ritchey had been named Miss Carlton, and Gladys Wills and Karl Stuckenberg were crowned Queen and King of the Centennial. The celebrations themselves included ball games, carnival rides, pony rides, a rodeo, a Fun Run, mud wrestling, an auction, exhibits of various kinds, a pancake breakfast, free cokes and sloppy joes, and a grand parade led by the VFW honor guard. All this was topped with a fly-over by the Air National Guard from Duluth. It was a festive commemoration of Carlton's official founding in keeping with the Carlton tradition of grand occasions. Although the Centennial is long over, Carlton continues to keep the community involved in joyful festivities that bring people together. Carlton Daze, which had its origins in the 1950s, is held on the last weekend in July and features softball, golf, basketball, running marathons, crafts shows, auctions, bingo, theater, street food, street dances, various entertainments, and a grand parade. Near Christmas, a breakfast with Santa is held largely for

King and Queen of the Centennial, Karl Stuckenberg and Gladys Wills, take a turn on the dance floor at the standing room only coronation pagent on June 27, 1981.
Photo from *Carlton County Vidette*

A float in the Centennial Parade passes the VFW hall.

the children, yet it also rallies the community in the late autumn. On the second weekend in February there is Winterfest, which centers on an ice fishing contest on Chub Lake and also features a chili cook-off. This mid-winter holiday has its origins in the 1950s ice fishing contest at Chub Lake organized by the Chamber of Commerce. The Chamber also organizes an Annual Community Banquet on the first Saturday in April for the specific purpose of honoring members of the community for outstanding achievements or contributions. The banquet encourages people to get together as winter's grip begins to ease. As it has been for fifty years, the Carlton calendar is full.

The past decades have given the people of Carlton and the surrounding area a steadily improved quality of life. The streets were resurfaced, the sidewalks repaired, the drinking water purified and the waste systems brought up to standard. A new post office, elementary school, print shop, VFW Club, a water treatment plant, a hockey arena, and county jail were built. Many older buildings were remodeled, like the Civic Center, and made available to new businesses or activities. A city park was created in town named

A new city park provides picnic facilities within sight of the business district of Carlton.   Photo by Tim Johnson

after a town pioneer Tom McFarland, a county park was created at Chub Lake, opening up the nearby lake to swimmers, picnickers, and boaters once again, and a private KOA campground and restaurant was built north of Carlton near the old Great Northern tracks. As the Burlington Northern Railroad consolidated its traffic on just a few of the competing sets of tracks and abandoned the rest, wonderful trails were created along those rights-of-way giving walkers and bikers easy access to some of the most beautiful country in the region. The Willard Munger State Trail has been planned to extend along the old Northern Pacific track from St. Paul to Duluth, and runs right through Carlton. The St. Louis River immediately below the Thomson Dam has become a choice area for white water kayak competitions. Carlton describes itself as the "Gateway to Jay Cooke State Park," but there are also many other choices of recreation spots in the area.

The building of I-35 did tend to cut Carlton off from the flow of traffic between the Twin Cities and the north. However, the area around the junction of the Interstate and Highways 210, 61, and 33, began to develop into a suburban community, itself linked to Carlton. What had originally been limited to Olson's Motel, became "Olsonville," a series of gas stations, restaurants, motels, and trucking firms. This was perhaps climaxed with the building of the Black Bear Casino, Hotel, and Golf Course, which created an up-scale entertainment center in a space that had been one of the original gravel pits for the Northern Pacific and the Zenith Gravel Company. Not actually part of Carlton, but something of a new suburb.

The 11th hole of the championship 18-hole Black Bear Golf Course.

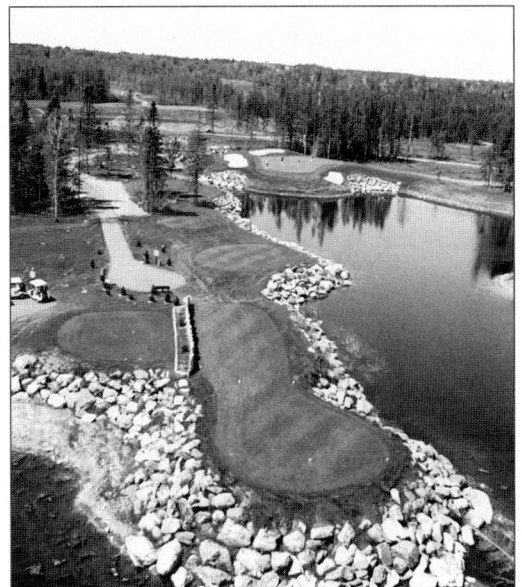

The Black Bear Casino, Hotel, and Golf Course provides economic benefits and entertainment to the Carlton area. Work has begun on a new casino building and an addition to the hotel complex which will further expand the Fond du Lac Reservation's business growth. Photos by Rocky Wilkinson, courtesy of the Fond du Lac Band of Lake Superior Chippewa

The leaders of the Carlton community in the 1960s could see in the evolving nature of the railroads and the building of the freeway system, that the old economic basis of the town would have to change. To meet that challenge Leonard A. Wilson, Jr., the village attorney, urged the creation of the Carlton Projects, Inc., in 1962. Its purpose would be to seek out and bring to Carlton, business or industry that would strengthen the economic base of the town and provide employment for its residents. The CPI raised $54,000 from local investors in order to qualify for larger amounts of money that could be made available through the Federal Area Redevelopment Administration, a government agency set up to help communities infuse new life into their local economies. Through the efforts of Senators Hubert H. Humphrey and Eugene McCarthy and Congressman John A. Blatnik, the government funding became available and a group of entrepreneurs were attracted. In March of 1964 the Carlton Machined Products moved into its new 20,000 foot building south of the Carlton Feed Mill. With elaborate and sophisticated machinery the CMP made finely machined parts for government contracts as well as for Honeywell, Minnesota Mining and Manufacturing, International Business Machines, and the local mills in Cloquet. The president of the company was James E. Parker of Minneapolis, the vice president Tom Young of Chub Lake, the secretary Roger Griffis of Minneapolis, and the treasurer G.L. Stewart of Cloquet; the directors similarly were a mixture of entrepreneurs and local investors. The firm expected to hire about one hundred skilled workers. Eventually CMP was succeeded by Stearns, Incorporated, which occupied the same building but manufactured safety gear, such as anti-exposure coveralls, flotation jackets, life vests, and rain suits. Currently the facility houses Jact's Express, a wholesale food trucking business, the Carlton Storage Company, and the Carlton County Soil and Water Conservation District offices.

The building of the Carlton Nursing Home in the 1950s was a major accomplishment for the town and its leaders. It was a gesture in anticipation of the demographics of the later twentieth century. With an aging population growing in number as the years moved forward, Carlton was well poised to become a center in the region for senior living. In 1962 plans were announced to expand the facility to create ten single rooms and twenty-five double rooms. Two years later the non-profit corporation that ran the facil-

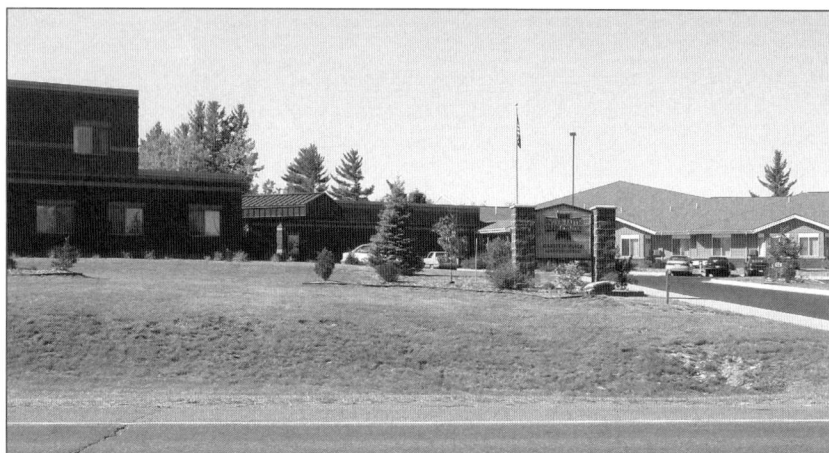

Carlton Inter-Faith Care Center with Carlton Place assisted living apartments on the right.   Photo by Tim Johnson

ity sold it to Mr. and Mrs. Bernard Buchanan. They expanded the complex, adding a series of assisted living apartments in an adjacent building. More recently the complex has been taken over by a consortium of six local churches. A new building completed in 2001 on the west side of Third Street has created an elaborate "campus" of facilities, now consisting of the Inter-Faith Care Center, a ninety-six bed nursing facility, Carlton Place, an assisted living structure, and Pine View Apartments, a comfortable, modern seniors residence. A child care center and meals-on-wheels program is also located there and the Liberalis treatment facility is located in the "old" nursing home building. Altogether, these resources make Carlton a major center for seniors and social services in the region.

This development highlights the dramatic shift in the Carlton economy, away from the heavy industry of the lumber trade, the railroads, and the oil refinery (which closed in 1982). It even shifted away from the traditional pattern of retail merchandising of consumer goods—the sale of men's and women's clothing, dry goods, hardware, kitchenware, appliances, and automobiles that, throughout much of the nineteenth and twentieth centuries, served as the driving force of every small town economy. The automobile, the freeway, the shopping mall, and the big box store have pretty well put an end to the traditional small town retail stores. However, the automobile and the freeway have made it possible for people who work in a metropolis to live or vacation in the rural parts of the country. Eventually they need services—builders, repairmen, automotive mechanics, heating and air conditioner experts, barbers and hair dressers, artists and craft suppliers, well diggers and septic tank cleaners, not to mention the more traditional services of doctors, dentists, lawyers. Carlton can provide all of these services, in addition to entertainment, restaurants, and bars to both people living in the town and those from the surrounding area.

Charles and Ann Dahlberg enter the St. Francis of Assisi Parish Center before the first mass in the new church.
Photo courtesy of Donna Melin

One area in which Carlton has traditionally provided services within the county has been as the seat of government. As Maurice Haubner observed, "People from every part of the county sooner or later visit the courthouse." Between the traditional functions of the county government and the regulations and services of the modern state, it is probably true that every property owner, tax payer, business person, builder, veteran, person in distress, or person in trouble with the law, must visit the Carlton County Courthouse. In addition to the district court, which is only periodically in session, there are all the offices of the county government and several of the state government— the County Commissioners, the Assessor, the Auditor/Treasurer, the Attorney, the Sheriff's Office, Public Health and Human Services, Emergency Management, the Highway Department, the Motor Vehicles Department, the Land Department, the Planning and Zoning Department, the Registrar of Titles, the Veterans Service, the Extension Service of the University of Minnesota, and more.

The new Carlton County Law Enforcement Center.
Photo by Tim Johnson

Carlton's past has partaken of many of the main themes of American and Minnesota history—exploration, settlement, railroad building, the forest industry, the farming frontier, the modern economy—and Carlton has carved out a secure place for itself in the life of the region. All roads in the county lead to the courthouse and to Carlton, now, just as they have done for one hundred and twenty-five years.

Sources:
Carlton County Vidette, 75th Anniversary Edition, February 24, 1964.
Carlton Minnesota Centennial. Carlton, 1981.

Jan Grannes

Not originally from Carlton, Jan Grannes was born in Montevideo, Minnesota, on April 27, 1937, and graduated from Breckenridge High School. She earned a Bachelor of Science degree from Concordia College and taught school at Canby and Brooklyn Park, Minnesota, where she served on the Parks and Recreation Commission. In 1975 she moved to Carlton where her husband ran a hardware store. Building on her Parks Commission experience, Grannes ran for Mayor of Carlton in 1977. Grannes was the first woman elected mayor. In her new office her first major task was to see the new water treatment plant project through to completion, followed by the building of the new fire hall and the opening of a city park. These large projects successfully undertaken, Grannes was sufficiently popular with the community to be elected six times. Grannes was also a member and officer of the Carlton Nursing Home, the AFS, the Carlton Chamber of Commerce, and the Carlton County Historical Society, of which she was president from 1991-1994. The Grannes family moved to Iowa in 2000.

Jan Grannes was Carlton's first woman mayor, and successfully guided the community through several ambitious projects.
Photo courtesy of Jan Grannes

The South Terrace Elementary School and play grounds in 2006.
Photo by Tim Johnson

CARLTON CHRONICLES
~ PEOPLE ~ PLACES ~ EVENTS

CARLTON, MINN.

Postcards from Carlton ~

Top - dated 1915
Courtesy of Tim Johnson

Middle - dated 1909

Bottom - around 1940
Courtesy of Barb Schmidt

The Matson home on 2nd Street.

Photo courtesy of Bob Anderson

The birthplace of Della Scheils Smith on March 10, 1894.

Photo courtesy of Barb Schmidt

This house was originally owned by the Paine family and was built by Eric Olaf (E.O) and Oscar Lycander.

Photo by Oscar Lycander, courtesy of Betty Lycander Peterson

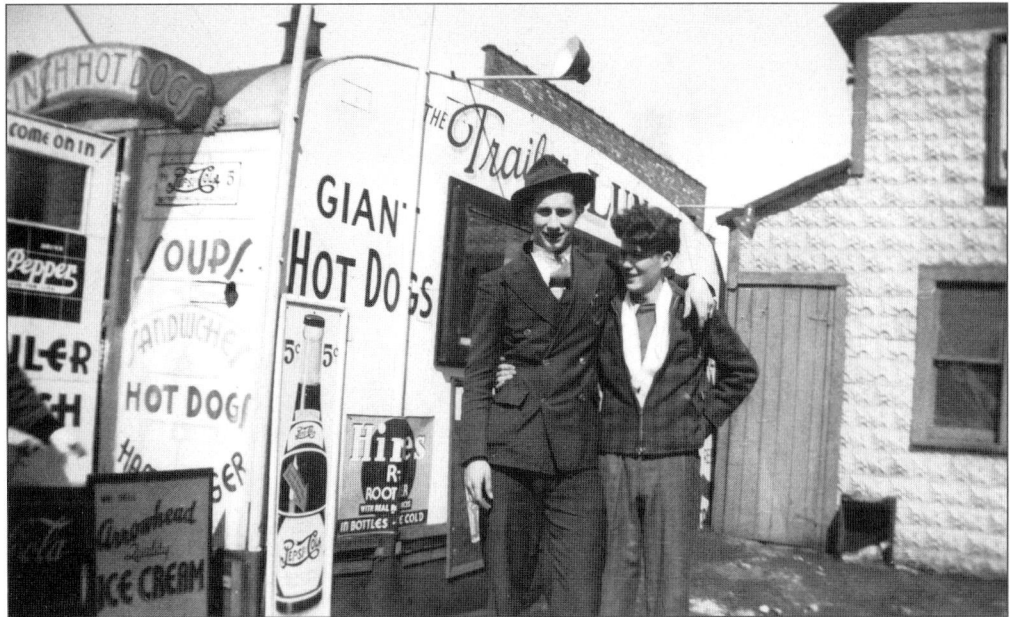

Frank Stine and Daryl Bradford at the hot dog trailer in 1937.

Photo courtesy of Leonard Stine

The National Tea Company building collapsed during the excavations for the building of a basement in the Street Car Café next door. Much of the goods and produce was moved across the street and the National Tea Company was more or less back in business the next day. But much had to be sorted out and a new building constructed.

Although still in the same place, the bank in Carlton has undergone many changes. Now the Wells Fargo Bank, the Carlton National Bank shown here was originally the First National Bank of Carlton.

The first and second grade Carlton Teeny Weeny Band in 1930-31.

Photo courtesy of Tim Johnson

Richard Anderson aboard the Farmall about 1952.

Photo courtesy of Barbara Gravelle

Men on a mission:
Pete Pierson
Jerry Granley
Michael Haubner
Grant Klosner
Dick Bergman
Jim Haubner.

Photo courtesy of Delphi Oswell

A grade school group: Nancy Kavanaugh, Allen Soukkala, Perry Coughlin, Karen Curtis, Kathy Bergstrom, Alvin Bryant.

Standing in front of the Post Office, "Happy" Clark, Sherman Liimatainen, and Gerald Bergum prepare to deliver papers sometime in the 1950s.

The Carlton graduating class of 1959. Back row: Dennis Bjork, Nona Habhegger, Joanne Zacher, Barbara J. Anderson, Barbara E. Anderson, Beverly Metso, Helen Ellsworth, Barbara Hargest, and Arthur Rask. Center row: Doris Rasmussen, William Anton, Al Ninteman, Robert Hargest, Roy Olson, Rawlston Rutter, Michael Haubner, Douglas Anderson, and Jeanette Munter. Front row: Richard Paulson, Barry Collins, Wayne Larson, Fred North, John Pierson, Donald Brown, Roger Jones, and Ronald Martini.

Wilbert Woodworth, ca. 1918.

Elizabeth Hewett Watkins, 1899.

Dr. J. D. Gilbert, 1948.

Alma Walters, long-time Carlton store owner.

Chester Beck, town constable from the 1930s to 1950s. Photo courtesy of Myrt Whelen

William Fall, Carlton Policeman.

Bertha and John Duffy, ca. 1940s. photo courtesy of Mike Duffy

Jewell Anderson, first Director of the Carlton County Historical Society, 1989. Photo courtesy of Barb Gravelle

Frank Ambrozich, long-time Principal of Carlton High School, served as Mayor of Carlton.

The Rennquist twins— Linda and Louise. Photo courtesy of Prudence Truman

The Newby twins, Jean and Jane, downtown.

Frank Stine and Bob Smith at the National Tea Store. Photo courtesy of Leonard Stine

Cliff Haubner and Don Ervin.

Photo courtesy of Tim Johnson

Ben and Al Johnson went fishing, ca. 1919. Photo courtesy of Tim Johnson

Willie Dengler with a 1924 Model T Ford.

Finley Palmer

Dick Duffy

Bob Schultz gets the keys to his "new" used car from John Duffy and Mr. Beseman at Duffy Motors in 1958.
Photo courtesy of Mike Duffy

Mr. Nicholson with an unidentified child, Duane "Tukey" Johnson, and Hughy Lane in front of Charlotte's Café.

Barber Carl Pierson. Photo courtesy of Peter Pierson

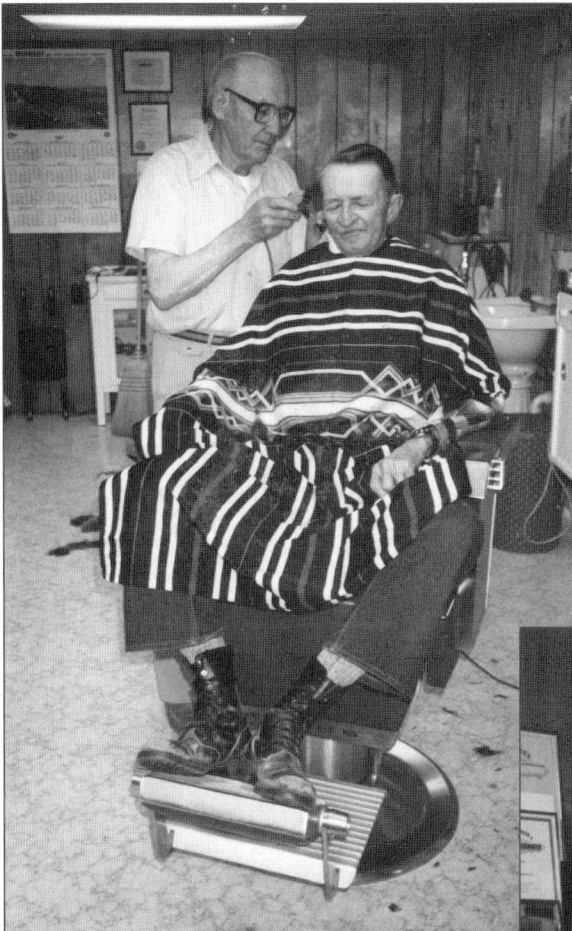
C. O. Williams barbered in Carlton from 1926 until 1996. Here he gives a haircut to Harold Wolf.
Photo courtesy of Darold Powers

Employees at Charlotte's Cafe—Frances McFall, Lorraine Carpenter, and Esther Johnson—help Charlotte Zacher (left) celebrate her birthday in 1998.

Carlton County Commissioners,
1957:
Carl Strandberg
"Scottie" Keith
Howard Ross
Ed Himango
Willis Carlson, county auditor
Martin Kotiranta.

Board of Directors of City
National Bank of Carlton
pictured in the early
1960s:
Rodney Thompson
Odin H. Roberts
Maurice Haubner
Jerry Stewart
Diane Hoffmockel
Stuart Beck
C. Merle Olson
Girard Stewart.

Photo by Denny's courtesy
of Michael Haubner

A gathering of old
friends:
Dave Schultz
Don McLish
Leslie "Babe" Zacher
Albert Johnson
George Gillespie
Don Ervin
Bill Jaskari
Harry Newby
Jack Sheff.

Photo courtesy of Tim
Johnson

A gala dinner ~
Frances McClay
Charlotte Zacher
Ada Zacher
Ellen Zacher
Angie Stine
Dolly Horner.

Lions Club Officers, 1970s
Seated: Dale Pierson, 2nd VP
Richard Schierber
Russell Grover, President
Al Griffin, Secretary
Dutch Thornton, 3rd VP
Standing:
Donald Pearson, Past President
Ray Bryant, Lion Tamer
William Miesner
Robert Schultz
William Dens
Odin Roberts
William Reynolds.

All Class Reunion Committee, 1975
Brucella Spearing Gibson, Jewell Hinz Anderson,
Evelyn Roley Bergman, Jim Overlie, Ray Gibson, Jr.

DFL activist and Carlton resident, Gene Rennquist,
is pictured in 1991 with State Representative Mary
Murphy, U.S. Representative James Oberstar, and
State Senator Becky Lourey.

Photo by Prudence Truman

Jameson's BAR-B-Q was a popular spot in Olsonville. Frank Guss and Mr. Jameson cut-it-up in front. Above right, Frank Guss presides over the bar and cash register in 1942.

Photos courtesy of Darold Powers

It looks like "Happy Days" in front of the Standard Station for the Johnson family— Albert and Doris with Wendy and Tim—around 1958.

Photo courtesy of Tim Johnson

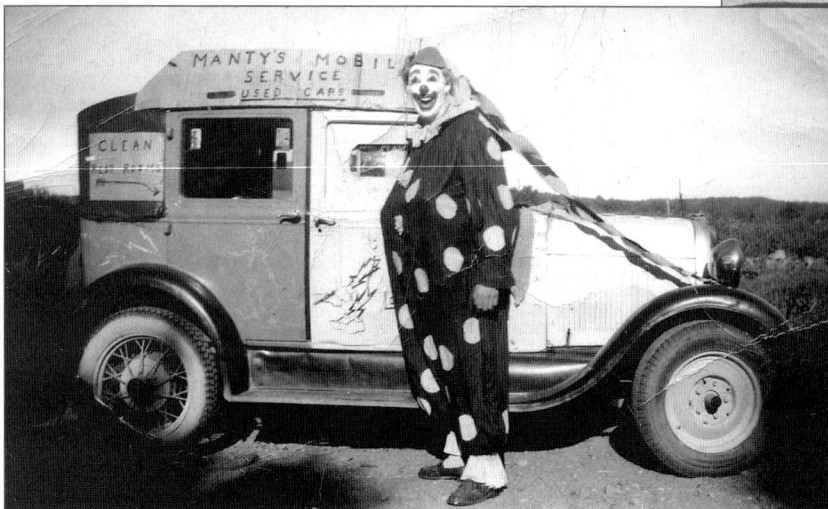

Gene Bro is just clowning around in the Manty's Mobile Service clown car.

Photo courtesy of Tim Johnson

Married in Carlton in 1925, Charles and Ann Dahlberg celebrated over 68 years of marriage.

Photos courtesy of Donna Melin

Posing at a family gathering in the 1950s are ~
Eleanor Hanson
Daisy Johnson
Elsie Matson Anderson
Edith Matson Lower
Sadie Johnson Ohearn
Sarah Johnson Holm.

Photo courtesy of Bob Anderson

Mayor Francis Roy and Fire Chief Stuart Beck rode in the U.S. Bicentennial parade in 1976 and see us to the end of our look at over 125 years of Carlton history.

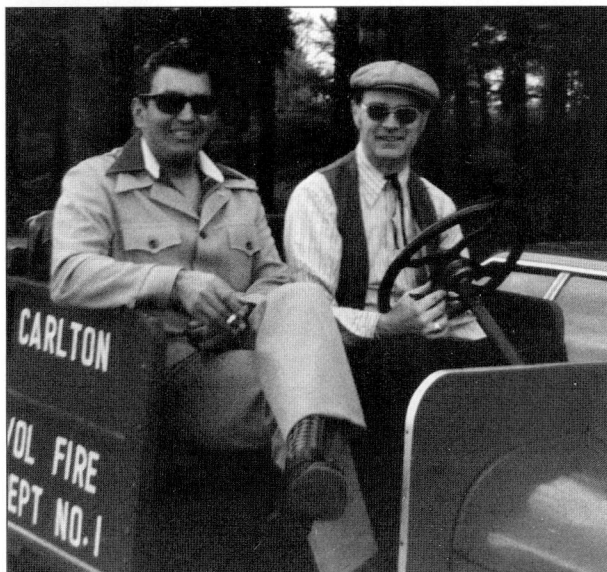

✑ SUGGESTED READINGS

There have been a number of books published about Carlton County history. Here is a list of some of the titles that are available for purchase at the Carlton County History & Heritage Center Store in Cloquet or from www.carltoncountyhs.org.

Beck, Bennett A. *Brief History of the Pioneers of the Cromwell, Minnesota Area.* Carlton County Historical Society, Cloquet, MN. 2001.

Carroll, Francis M. *Crossroads in Time: A History of Carlton County, Minnesota.* Carlton County Historical Society, Cloquet, MN. 1987.

Carroll, Francis M. and Franklin R. Raiter. *The Fires of Autumn: The Cloquet-Moose Lake Disaster of 1918.* Minnesota Historical Society Press, St. Paul, MN. 1990.

Carroll, Francis M. and Marlene Wisuri. *Reflections of Our Past: A Pictorial History of Carlton County, Minnesota.* Donning Company, Virginia Beach, VA. 1997.

Fahlstrom, Paul. *Anna Dickie and Peter Olesen: Notable Citizens of Cloquet.* Carlton County Historical Society, Cloquet, MN. 1996.

Fahlstrom, Paul. *Old Cloquet, Minnesota—White Pine Capitol of the World.* Gateway Press, Inc. Baltimore, MD. 1997.

1918 Fire Stories. Moose Lake Area Historical Society, Moose Lake, MN. 2003.

Luukkonen, Larry. *Cloquet: The Story Behind the Name.* Carlton County Historical Society, Cloquet, MN. 2000.

Luukkonen, Larry. *Reuben B. Carlton: Frontier Blacksmith and Visionary.* Carlton County Historical Society, Cloquet, MN. 2005.

Luukkonen, Larry and Marlene Wisuri. *A Hometown Album: Cloquet's Centennial Story.* Carlton County Historical Society, Cloquet, MN. 2004.

Mattinen, John A. translated by Richard Impola. *History of the Thomson Farming Area.* Carlton County Historical Society, Cloquet, MN. 2000.

O'Meara, Walter. *We Made It Through the Winter: A Memoir of Northern Minnesota Boyhood.* Minnesota Historical Society Press, St. Paul, MN. 1974.

Peacock, Thomas D. (ed.). *A Forever Story: The People and Community of the Fond du Lac Reservation.* Fond du Lac Band of Lake Superior Chippewa, Cloquet, MN. 1998.

Petersen Kurt (ed.). *Stories of a Century: Cloquet Centennial Book of Reflections 1904 - 2004.* Carlton County Historical Society and the Cloquet Centennial Committee, Cloquet, MN. 2004.

Skalko, Christine and Marlene Wisuri. *Fire Storm: The Great Fires of 1918.* Carlton County Historical Society, Cloquet, MN. 2003.

Swanson, S. Hjalmar. *A History of Mahtowa: With Additional Material by Willie Newman.* Carlton County Historical Society, Cloquet, MN. 2005.

Photo by Harriette Niemi

Timothy Johnson, a life-long Carlton resident, has chaired the Carlton History Committee and is on the Board of Directors of the Carlton County Historical Society. He retired as Manager of Locomotive Maintenance for the Duluth Missabe & Iron Range Railroad. He has a keen interest in local history, especially railroad history, and is currently enjoying some travel, camping and fishing.

Francis M. Carroll is originally from Cloquet and Chub Lake. He was educated at Carleton College, the University of Minnesota, and Trinity College Dublin, and he is currently Professor Emeritus of History at the University of Manitoba. This is his tenth book, including three of Carlton County history— *Crossroads in Time*, *The Fires of Autumn*, with Franklin R. Raiter, and *Reflections of Our Past*, with Marlene Wisuri.

Marlene Wisuri is the Director of the Carlton County Historical Society and holds an M.F.A. degree from the University of Massachusetts. She has previously co-authored eight books including three books of Ojibwe culture and history with Thomas Peacock and two books about the Finnish immigrant experience with Jim Johnson. Her photographs have appeared in numerous exhibitions.